When facing a trial, nowhere is the Christian calling to 'fake it 'til you make it.' In *A Heart Set Free*, Christina Fox invites us to vulnerability, transparency and trust – particularly when life is hard. She does so by walking us through the often avoided Psalms of Lament, those dark and blustery passages whose presence in the Bible unsettles us. Christina offers practical, empathetic help for those whose emotions have taken them captive in a time of upheaval, tracing a biblical pattern for lamenting to God with honesty, trust and worship. No need to hide our sorrows and fears. Our Father leans close to hear the cries of His children.

Jen Wilkin
Author of *Women of the Word: How to Study the Bible with Both Our Hearts and Mind*

We're emotional creatures, whether we stuff our emotions deep down in there or let them take the lead. I wish I had Christina's book back when I became a believer. It would have saved me a lot of painful emotion-stuffing and foolish emotion-ignoring. Read this one slowly, plan to discuss it with a friend, and anticipate a season of worship-driven reflection on God's faithfulness to you.

Gloria Furman
Author of *Glimpses of Grace, Treasuring Christ When Your Hands Are Full*, and *The Pastor's Wife*

We typically hear that we should either stuff our emotions and get over ourselves, or that we should give full vent to our emotions and live what we feel. In *A Heart Set Free*, Christina Fox comes at our emotions, particularly the emotion of lament, from a biblical view. Using the Psalms she takes the reader on a valuable journey teaching how to understand and express our emotions to our Heavenly Father. I am grateful for her work on this book and I am confident it will be a great help to many people.

Jessica Thompson
Speaker and author of *Answering Your Kid's Toughest Questions* and *Everyday Grace: Infusing all Your Relationships with the Love of Jesus*

Christina shows us from God's Word the importance of trusting Jesus with our emotions, even when we are weeping. With theological integrity and practical suggestions she tenderly teaches us the language of lament and how our lamentations can take us to the gospel.

Susan Hunt
Pastor's wife, former Director of Women's Ministry for the PCA,
speaker, and author of more than a dozen books
for women and children, including *Spiritual Mothering:
The Titus 2 Model for Women Mentoring Women*

Some days feel like a roller coaster ride – up and down, and if possible sideways. It's because our emotions are real. Christina helps us face the facts – we have emotions but we don't have to be lost on that roller coaster ride and neither must we give in. Christina doesn't ignore our emotions, rather she drives us from the wild ride to the freedom found in Jesus.

Trillia Newbell
Author of *Fear and Faith* and *United*

The undertow of our emotions can quickly sweep us away. *A Heart Set Free* anchors our hearts in the truth and invites us to cry out boldly to our Savior.

Karen Hodge
Women's Ministry Coordinator for the Presbyterian Church in America

A wonderful book that uncovers the realities of our emotions and gives us a theological framework for understanding them. It reminds us constantly to review the gospel story in our hearts. Christina Fox is really practical about how to articulate our emotions to God. And rather than letting emotions control us, we learn how they can focus our hearts more firmly on God in the midst of all life's deepest troubles.

Ursula Weekes
Minister's Wife at Emmanuel Church Wimbledon in London

A Heart Set Free

A JOURNEY TO HOPE
THROUGH
THE PSALMS OF
LAMENT

Christina Fox

CHRISTIAN
FOCUS

Unless otherwise stated Scripture quotations are from *The Holy Bible, English Standard Version*, copyright © 2001 by Crossway Bibles, a division of Good News Publishers. Used by permission. All rights reserved. ESV Text Edition: 2007.

Scripture quotations marked RSV are taken from *The Revised Standard Version of the Bible*, copyright 1952 [2nd edition, 1971] by the Division of Christian Education of the National Council of the Churches of Christ in the United States of America. Used by permission. All rights reserved.

Christina Fox received her undergraduate degree from Covenant College and her Master's in Counseling Psychology from Palm Beach Atlantic University. She writes for a number of Christian ministries and publications including Desiring God Ministries and The Gospel Coalition. She lives with her husband and two sons in sunny South Florida. She chronicles her faith journey at www.christinafox.com.

Copyright © Christina Fox 2016

paperback ISBN: 978-1-78191-728-2
epub ISBN: 978-1-78191-729-9
mobi ISBN: 978-1-78191-730-5

10 9 8 7 6 5 4 3 2

Published in 2016
by
Christian Focus Publications Ltd,
Geanies House, Fearn,
Ross-shire, IV20 1TW, Scotland.
www.christianfocus.com

Cover design by Paul Lewis

Printed by Bell and Bain, Glasgow

CONTENTS

Foreword

When Paul wrote to his beloved Philippians, he told them, 'For I have learned in whatever situation I am to be content. I know how to be brought low, and I know how to abound. In any and every circumstance, I have learned the secret of facing plenty and hunger, abundance and need. I can do all things through him who strengthens me' (Phil. 4:11b-13).

Throughout the years, I have pondered these words, longing to share in this secret with Paul, wanting to know Christ in such a way that inner joy abounds whatever the outward circumstance. And, most of the time, I have found myself wrestling with my emotions along the way.

At times, I wrongly viewed contentment as an emotional evenness that nothing could assuage. So, when emotions would arise such as sadness, anger, frustration, or grief, these were signs of my failure. If I felt too much enjoyment in the things of this earth, I viewed these emotions with suspicion. Perhaps my joy, gladness, and delight were signs of misplaced affections.

My quest for contentment often led me to try and avoid my emotions. Yet, each time I tried to push them down, they would pop back up in another form. In some ways, I found myself struggling with the fact that I had any negative emotions at all. Wasn't I supposed to 'Rejoice always, pray without ceasing, give thanks in all circumstances; for this is the will of God in Christ Jesus for you'(1 Thess. 5:16-18)? Did this verse leave room for sorrow, fear, anxiety, or grief?

In the midst of my inward debate, life kept happening. We suffered a miscarriage, my father had a heart attack and stroke, my mother faced cancer and months of treatment, and a dear friend died after a long fight with breast cancer. Where was I to go with the pain and loss I was feeling?

In my wrestling and thinking, my husband lovingly and faithfully nudged me back into God's Word: 'Melissa, you need to go to the Psalms.'

I followed his advice and found words to express both my sorrows and my joys. The Psalms expanded my view of God, as well as my view of contentment. Here I found saints who were living before me, displaying what it meant to be 'sorrowful, yet rejoicing' (2 Cor. 6:10). In the Psalms I learned that sadness and grief were not signs of faithlessness, but part of life in a fallen world. Grief could walk beside joy and they were not in opposition to one another. Contentment was not an avoidance of emotions, but a God-centered expression of them.

In the Psalms I found a pattern for how to talk to myself. As Martyn Lloyd-Jones wrote, 'You have to take yourself in hand, you have to address yourself, preach to yourself, question yourself.' The Psalms provided examples of saints who faithfully wrestled with God as they poured out their souls before Him. Their emotions drove them to closer to God, in a new dependence upon Him.

These meditations refreshed and renewed my love of the Psalms. For this reason, when Christina Fox told me that she was working on a book on emotions and the Psalms, I rejoiced. In this book she faithfully nudges us all back to the Psalms, with wisdom and discernment as she guides. She does so through the lens of her own experience, with her eyes firmly focused on Christ.

Christina wisely helps us to understand our emotions and faithfully teaches the pattern of lament found in the Psalms. She directs us to cry out to God, ask Him for help, and to respond in trust and worship. She leads us into the experience of our emotions, but away from self-focus and self-pity. She is tender and truthful, blending a sympathetic heart with a theological mind.

I am thankful this book has reached your hands. I pray that it might encourage you to join with the saints of old, crying out to the Lord in your distress. May we experience Him in new ways as we seek Him in all things.

Be merciful to me, O God, be merciful to me,
     for in you my soul takes refuge;
in the shadow of your wings I will take refuge,
     till the storms of destruction pass by.
I cry out to God Most High,
     to God who fulfills his purpose for me. (Ps. 57:1-2)

Blessings,

Melissa Kruger
Author of *The Envy of Eve: Finding Contentment in a Covetous World* and *Walking with God in the Season of Motherhood*

Acknowledgments

It was half-time at my son's soccer game. The coach gathered all the kids together in a circle around him. He looked at my son and said, 'How many goals did you get?' 'One,' my son answered. 'You got two,' the coach responded. He looked at the next child. 'How many goals did you get?' 'Zero,' the boy said. 'You got two,' the coach said again. He asked each child the same question and responded to each answer with, 'You got two.' He then went on to tell them that it took each one of them working together as a team to get the ball down the field and into the goal. Even though one child made the kick that scored a goal, it was really all of them who earned the goal.

I feel the same way about the process of writing a book. My name might be on the cover, but there is a whole team of people behind me who helped me in the process of writing it.

First, I am so thankful to the Lord for providing the opportunity to write this book. Without His sovereign hand and care over this project, it would not have come to fruition. This book is a testimony to His work in my life and an affirmation that joy does indeed come in the morning. Each day I am amazed by His generous grace for me in Christ and wonder-struck by His daily provision of mercy. I pray that He would use this book for His glory and fame.

I'd like to extend a special thank you to Melissa Kruger for connecting me with Christian Focus Publications. Melissa, thank you for your generous spirit, encouragement, and prayers throughout this project. Christian Focus is a delightful group of godly believers to work with and I am incredibly grateful for the opportunity to work with them. I am especially thankful to the kindness of Kate MacKenzie and her diligent work in acquiring my manuscript. Thank you, Kate for your encouragement and guidance. Willie MacKenzie, thank you for your patience and kindness toward me as I made my way through this new and unfamiliar territory of book publication. And a big thanks to Anne Norrie for your editorial work and encouragement during the editing process.

I had several friends read through the manuscript for me, helping me work through the kinks and point out things I missed: Tara Barthel, Lisa Tarplee, and Randy Wallin. Tara, your editorial insights were invaluable as were your prayers and wisdom as an experienced writer. I am blessed by your friendship. Thank you, Lisa, for your constant friendship, prayers, and listening ear throughout this process. I could not have done this without you! Randy, your theological wisdom, kindness, and constant encouragement spurred me on to keep reading, studying, and writing.

I am thankful to my fellow writing friends and mentors who have been a great source of wisdom, guidance, and encouragement: Gloria Furman, Maryanne Helms, Trillia Newbell, Ashleigh Slater, Jessica Thompson, and Jen Wilkin. Thanks also to my online writing friends at WWWS. I've learned so much from you all as we spur one another on in our writing and faithfulness to the Word of truth. Thank you to Karen Hodge for your help, encouragement, and guidance in my writing ministry.

Thank you, Collin Hansen, and the editors at The Gospel Coalition for accepting that first article I submitted. I have learned so much from your ministry and am grateful for your interest in my work. Thank you to Desiring God Ministries and the editors I have worked with there: Jonathan Parnell, Tony Reinke, and Marshall Segal. Because of your editing, encouragement, and guidance, I have grown and continue to grow as a writer. I am especially thankful to John Piper for providing the opportunity for me to write for his ministry and for his faithful pursuit in pointing us to the source of all joy: Jesus Christ. Thank you also to the editors at iBelieve, ERLC, CBMW, Aquila Report, True Woman, Gospel Mag, and For the Family, for sharing my writing with your readers. Thanks to my blog readers for their support and encouragement. Thank you for reading my posts and for your kind and generous feedback.

I extend thanks also to my friends, family, and church family at TCPC who faithfully prayed with and for me during this process: Lisa Tarplee, Marilyn Southwick, Kerri Trice, Cara Leger, Christy Richardson, Miriam Gautier, Tiffany Bone, Misha Harris, John and Linda Swisher, Judy Fox, Steve and Pauline Apperson, Shanna Fox and Sabrina Carr. Thank you for your love, encouragement, and support. A special thanks to my pastor, David Richardson. Your faithful preaching of the gospel has fed me week after week with the richest of foods. I couldn't thank you enough for your diligence and wisdom to point me to Christ. I also couldn't have written a single word without the constant help of my babysitter, Karen Mitchell. Thanks so much for loving my boys!

And far from least, I am so thankful to my husband George and our boys, Ethan and Ian. They are my prayer warriors. Without their support pushing me forward, I could not have done this. Thank you, George, for believing in me, for carrying me when I needed it, for loving me in my darkest days, and for encouraging me to write. Thank you, Ethan and Ian, for your patience and love and for the joy it is to be your mother. I love you all!

Christina Fox

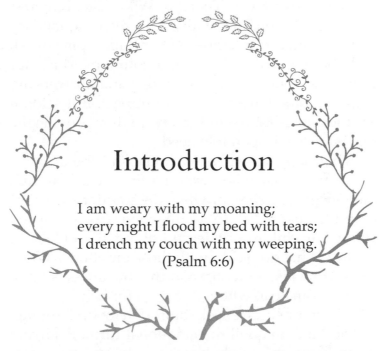

Introduction

I am weary with my moaning;
every night I flood my bed with tears;
I drench my couch with my weeping.
(Psalm 6:6)

Emotions. They are common to everyone. If you are human, then you are an emotional being. Some emotions are pleasant, like happiness, contentment, and excitement. Others are burdensome and bear down heavy, like sorrow, shame, worry, and envy. For some of us, negative emotions can be fleeting and for others they are constant companions. They can rule our days, govern our choices, and steal our joy. What's more, we know we shouldn't be slaves to our emotions but we just don't know what to do with them. Do we reject them? Try to never experience them? Give in to them?

We live in an age where there is a quick fix to every problem. Answers to our questions are found at the strike of a key. There's a Wiki page, Pinterest board, and YouTube video for every quandary or issue we can imagine. We can like, pin, tweet, and share countless ideas and solutions to all our problems. Some of those solutions and answers are helpful. Some indeed make an impact. But seldom are they long-lasting and rarely do they provide the real hope we desperately need.

What happens when we don't find the answers to our problems, when we can't find peace through our Google searches, or when the solutions we have found fail us? What do we do when we are worried about our children or fearful about the unknown future? What do we do with those emotions? When the sorrow just won't lift and the loneliness is more than we can bear, where do we go for help?

For some of us, we seek comfort in food, shopping, or Facebook to quell the emotional turmoil stirring in our hearts. We might busy ourselves with projects or work long hours to keep our mind off our pain. We might look at our circumstances and seek to change our situation in the hope that we will finally feel at peace once our life has changed.

The truth is, there are many ways we seek relief from the pains and problems of this life and there are many sources that seek to sell us the solution to all our problems. But the question I want to raise to you is, in the midst of all your painful emotions, how often do you look to God in His Word for help and hope? How often do you turn to Him when you feel anxious, distraught, or abandoned? How often do you bring your burdens to your Savior?

God's Word, in particular the Psalms, is a rich resource for help when we are hurting. They provide comfort and hope. In fact, the Psalms, especially the Psalms of Lament, give us a structure for how to express our feelings. They remind us what is true. They point us to God's love and faithfulness. They help us journey through the dark valleys until we can emerge on the other side and bow in grateful worship.

What You Can Expect From This Book

The purpose of this book is to help us face the reality of our emotions. Instead of hiding them, distracting ourselves from them, or avoiding them, we are going to face them head on. We are going to walk right into the pain. We are going to learn how to express our emotions and bring them before our loving Heavenly Father.

In this book, we are going on a journey to find Christ as the healer of all the wounds in our soul. We are going to see how His redemption applies not only to our salvation from sin, but also to our daily struggles with emotions. This book will point us to the hope we have in Christ. It will point us away from the ways in which we normally handle our emotions and to the truth of God's Word. It will draw us deeper into God's grace where we'll find our rest in Him as our Savior.

The writers of the laments felt many of the same emotions we feel. They went through a journey with their emotions and we will follow their journey. We will go through the steps of the laments with worship as the ultimate goal.

What You Can't Expect From This Book

There are a few things you should not expect from this book. This book does not presuppose that there is never a physiological element to our emotions that requires some kind of medical treatment. We are not entirely spiritual beings, nor are we entirely physical beings. We are both, and as such there is a complex relationship between the two when it comes to our emotions. The effects of the fall are far reaching and we feel its effect in our entire being, including our physical bodies. However, it is beyond the scope of this book to address the physical issues because our focus in this book is on the Psalms of Lament.

Additionally, the lessons learned in this book are not meant to be used in isolation or apart from any other counseling or treatment. This book is not meant to be a replacement for counseling. It can, however, serve as an aid and work in conjunction with counseling. So if you are one who is enslaved by your emotions, please do not read this book in lieu of wise and godly counsel.

If you are looking for a book that gives you ten steps to making your life all you've ever wanted, this is not the book for you. If you are looking for a book that will tell you how to rid your life of painful emotions forever, this is not the book for you. If you are looking for a magic formula, cure-all, or another thing to add to a spiritual to-do list, this is not the book for you.

This book is not a how-to book, but you will find some practical steps to apply what you are learning in the Psalms. This book is also not a traditional Bible study, but it does encourage you to read through the Psalms of Lament. I provide passages for you to read and questions for you to think about and consider at the end of each chapter.

Like most journeys in life, progressing through this book will not be a race, but more of a marathon that you set at your own pace. Take your time as you go through the chapters. Unpack your bags and stay with one for a while. Spend time with the psalmists and seek to learn from the laments.

Thank you for joining me in this journey.

PART 1

Emotional Captors
and
Freedom
in Christ

1

Unwanted Guests

Have you ever had unwelcome visitors in your home? Maybe they were initially welcome, but then they stayed longer than they should have? You know the kind, the ones who suck your energy, demand all your time, and leave you weary and worn.

I've had a frequent visitor in my life since adolescence. Sometimes I know in advance when he will arrive. Other times he shows up without any notice at all. When he's there, he consumes everything in my life. He leaves me exhausted and spent. A few times, he's even brought friends along for a visit and when they all finally leave, it looks like a tornado touched down and left only destruction in its wake.

You'd think we would be close friends, considering all the time we've spent together. But we're not. I actually don't consider him a friend at all and I'd like to sever our relationship once and for all. You may or may not have met him, for my visitor – whom I call Despair – spends much of his time down deep in my heart.

Do you have a frequent visitor in your life? Perhaps instead of Despair, you visitor might go by the name of Shame or Anger, Fear or Anxiety. Maybe you have a visitor that disguises his intentions for a while, masquerading as someone else, perhaps someone who is useful and easy to hang around with. And then one day you wake up and find out who they really are and that they've settled in, making themselves at home. These visitors might go by the name Stress, Worry, Irritability, or Discontentment.

Hostages

The visitors I am speaking of are all emotions. While each of us has different emotions and differing degrees of such emotions, we all know what these difficult emotions are like. Sometimes they are brief and merely stop by for a cup of tea and then they are on their way. But for many of us, our emotions have taken up permanent residence and they aren't content to simply be a guest, they want to be landlords. They want full rights and free access to our hearts, telling us what we can and cannot do. The truth is, our emotions can take us hostage. They can paralyze us. Like a deer caught in the headlights of a car, we become immobilized in their presence. Emotions can consume us, rule us, and direct us. Like thieves, they steal our joy and peace.

Have you ever heard of the Stockholm syndrome? That is a term used to describe a psychological phenomenon that can happen when someone is held hostage. The hostage develops empathy and sympathy toward their captor and over time even develops positive feelings toward them, sometimes to the point of defending them. This can happen to us as well with our emotions. We start to think that Worry isn't so bad to have around. After all, he does clean up after himself and everyone else likes to have him over too. We get used to Stress and Despair, it seems like they are part of us. But these emotions are territorial. They like to have us all to themselves. As a result, the longer we live with them, the more joy and peace seem like a fading memory.

The Key of Promise

Are you familiar with the classic allegory *Pilgrim's Progress*? In this centuries-long best seller, a pilgrim named Christian goes on a journey from the City of Destruction to the Celestial City. It is an allegory of the Christian life. In his journey to the Celestial City, Christian is supposed to stay on the narrow path, but on one occasion he and his fellow traveling companion, Hopeful, wander off the path and end up at Doubting Castle. Giant Despair lives there and puts both Christian and Hopeful in a cage.

Day after day the Giant torments them. He taunts them and tells them they should just give up and end their life. Finally, since they won't do so, the Giant decides he will kill them himself. But before he gets the opportunity to do that, Christian remembers that he has the Key of Promise tucked away in his pocket. Once he remembers, he is able to open the door to the cage and they run back to the narrow path and onward to the Celestial City.

The story of Christian's journey in *Pilgrim's Progress* reminds us that we will encounter difficult emotions in our own journey of faith. We may even be captured and held captive by them. But it also reminds us that there is freedom and a way out. So what is the key of promise that Christian had that set him free from the torment of the Giant called Despair? It was the gospel and the hope we have through Jesus Christ.

As we begin this journey of facing our emotions and finding our own key of promise, let's start by exploring the various captors in our lives.

The Captors: Worry, Fear, and Anxiety
Emotions are common to the human condition. Some emotions, like happiness and contentment, are good and pleasant. We love those emotions and often go out of our way to invite them over for a weekend stay, hoping that perhaps they'll even want to move in for a while. But we all know that emotions like

happiness are fleeting, preferring instead to stay for a cup of coffee and then they are off again.

Sadly, the emotions that like to stay for lengthy visits are those we don't want to have around. Some are sneaky and hard to recognize, especially Worry. Worry often comes in disguise, making up some excuse as to why he stopped by. There's a storm on the horizon, a potential hazard up ahead, traffic is backed up, a virus is spreading around town, you name it, if it's something bad, Worry will stop by and tell us about it.

In fact, Worry, and its cousins Fear and Anxiety, not only like to stay for long visits, they also like to go on trips. These emotions love to do a bit of time traveling. Worry, fear, and anxiety live in the future. They anticipate and expect the worst. They imagine all sorts of bad scenarios and frightening outcomes. Usually they expect things to happen that rarely ever do. They keep us up at night, making our stomach tight and uneasy. Our minds are on constant alert, always watching out for that devastating event that lies just around the corner.

We usually think of our worries as harmless and normal. Everyone worries so we often don't even look at it as something we shouldn't do. Moms who don't worry about their husbands or kids are looked at as strange and uncaring. Worry is so common that when we women get together, we try to out-worry one another. We share our stories, our worries and stresses, and all the ways we are trying to get our life under control. We even give each other advice on how to worry more. 'Did you know that if you let your child do ____, ____ will happen?' 'I read recently that ____ can harm you. You should never buy____, use ___, eat ____, or take your children ____.'

When worry becomes a serious habit, it changes its name to Anxiety. Anxiety is such a problem in our society that statistics show that 18 per cent of American adults receive treatment for it.[1] Pharmaceutical companies are always coming out with new medications to treat anxiety, yet strangely enough, the number of patients only continues to grow.

When it comes to fear, we can fear anything. Spiders, heights, germs, snakes, airplanes, and even other people are on the list of common phobias. Fear paralyzes us. It keeps us from moving forward in life. It makes our heart race, our hands shake, and our feet stay in place.

Sometimes fear comes out of nowhere and is unexpected. I once went to an indoor rock-climbing place with my family. My kids weren't the only ones excited to strap in and climb the faux rock wall, I was too. Yet when I got to the top and looked down below me, I couldn't let go. I panicked. My grip tightened, my heart pounded, and my breath felt trapped in my throat. I called out for my husband but I couldn't get his attention. I knew I couldn't stay up there forever but I just couldn't let go. Fear held me there.

The Bible has a lot to say about all three emotions, worry, anxiety, and fear. Jesus said in Matthew 6:25,

---

1.   National Institute for Mental Health. 'Any Anxiety Disorder Among Adults.' http://www.nimh.nih.gov/statistics/1ANYANX_ADULT.shtml (accessed May 26, 2014).

'Therefore I tell you, do not be anxious about your life, what you will eat or drink, nor about your body, what you will put on. Is not life more than food, and the body more than clothing?' Paul said this about anxiety, 'Do not be anxious about anything, but in everything by prayer and supplication with thanksgiving let your requests be made known to God' (Phil. 4:6). After a fierce storm, Jesus said to the disciples, ' "Why are you afraid, O you of little faith?" Then he rose and rebuked the winds and the sea, and there was a great calm' (Matt. 8:26).

So while we may sometimes find worry, anxiety, and fear to be acceptable, even normal, Scripture does not. The Bible is clear that we should not worry, be anxious, or fearful. Easier said than done, right? Do any of these emotions hold you hostage? Have you grown comfortable with them taking up residence in your heart? Hold on to that answer as we look at a few more emotions.

Despair, Grief, and Sorrow
Let's face it, life is hard. The trials of life are many. Jesus said to His disciples, 'In this world you will have tribulation. But take heart; I have overcome the world' (John 16:33). Sorrow and grief are expected in this life. This is especially true for Christ's followers. Jesus warned us that following Him would be hard, even going so far as to tell us that we must bear our own crosses. 'Then Jesus told his disciples, "If anyone would come after me, let him deny himself and take up his cross and follow me"' (Matt. 16:24). We are told to expect persecution. We will face loss

and trials for Christ's sake. 'For to this you have been called, because Christ also suffered for you, leaving you an example, so that you might follow in his steps' (1 Pet. 2:21). But despite knowing that we can expect such sorrow and suffering, it doesn't make it any less painful when it comes.

Grief and sorrow enter our lives through loss and hardship. We lose a job, our house, or a loved one. We might grieve because of a marriage torn by divorce. Or maybe we grieve broken promises or unmet desires. Grief is a normal response to the death and decay prevalent in this broken world. The shortest verse in Scripture attests to the fact that Jesus expressed sorrow over the loss of His friend, Lazarus.

Sometimes though, when sorrow and grief linger, they grow into despair. Despair, often called depression, pulls us into a dark pit where the sun doesn't shine. We feel lost and alone. There's no hope of getting out. While the world continues to go on as usual, we live in isolation, with dark thoughts and tears as our only companions. Like the prophet Jeremiah, we may wish we had never been born (Jer. 15:10).

Despair can linger and make itself a permanent fixture in our life. It can ruin relationships and jobs. It keeps us from living life and serving others. Always jealous of our affections, it pulls us away from others, telling us that no one else cares. We could be standing in a crowd of people and feel like we are all alone in the world. In truth, despair is crippling and debilitating.

Despair and I have journeyed many years together. I first felt its tug on my heart the year my grandmother died, I switched schools, and lost close friends. I spent much of my adolescence hidden away in my room, crying and not knowing how to stop. Following the birth of my two children, Despair again made an appearance. It pushed me to the edge, so close that one day I wanted to drive right into a tree.

If you are familiar with sorrow, grief, or despair, it's hard to imagine life ever being normal again. It feels like you've been shoved into a locked cage with the key thrown away. But as the psalmist says, there is hope, 'Weeping may tarry for the night, but joy comes with the morning' (Ps. 30:5). Stay with me in this journey as we seek that morning sun.

Abandonment, Rejection, and Shame

I remember reading words of rejection from a friend. I had reached out to her with vulnerability. Her words of response cut deep and pierced my heart. I couldn't stop crying for the pain. It made me question who I was and my worth as a person. I recalled all our time together and questioned each of my memories. I couldn't get past it.

Sometimes rejection comes from someone we don't know well and is short-lived. Perhaps it comes from a potential employer. We are disappointed by their response but we move on. Other times it comes at the hand of a loved one and it leaves us reeling. It feels like it came out of nowhere. We were unprepared and defenseless. It rocked our known world so much that we couldn't imagine life ever being the same.

Our heart can relate to that of the psalmist, 'For it is not an enemy who taunts me—then I could bear it; it is not an adversary who deals insolently with me—then I could hide from him. But it is you, a man, my equal, my companion, my familiar friend' (Ps. 55:12-13).

Abandonment is similar and sometimes is intertwined with rejection. Perhaps a parent left you as a child. Or maybe a spouse left for greener pastures. Sometimes we can even feel abandoned by God. Feeling abandoned can lead to other emotions like fear and despair. The wounds of abandonment travel with us wherever we go, affecting future relationships and causing further heartache.

Shame is a heavy emotion that we wear like a second skin. It becomes our identity. It feels like all eyes are on us, all the time. It's like we are wearing a scarlet letter around our neck. Everyone knows who we are and what we did or what was done to us. Ed Welch describes shame as 'the deep sense that you are unacceptable because of something you did, something done to you, or something associated with you. You feel exposed and humiliated.'[2] He goes on, 'Hiding. Covering up. Self-protection. Feeling exposed. They are telltale signs of shame.'[3]

These are just some of the emotions that can come into our lives and take up residence. Perhaps your

---

2.   Welch, Ed. *Shame Interrupted: How God Lifts the Pain of Worthlessness and Rejection* (Greensboro, NC: New Growth, 2012), p. 2.

3.   Ibid., p. 46.

heart resonated with a few of them. That was the purpose of this chapter, to help you see the emotions in your life that hold you hostage. Don't despair, this was only Chapter 1. As we move along in this journey, we'll get closer to that key of promise that unlocks the door and sets your heart free.

For Your Heart

1. Take time to consider the emotions in your life. Are there specific ones that have moved in and ruled your life? What are they?

2. Read through the following passages and write down what Scripture says about emotions: Isaiah 43:5, Matthew 10:26-33, Proverbs 17:22, Revelation 21:4.

3. Pray and ask God to reveal to you the emotions that enslave you. Pray for wisdom and discernment to identify and face them.

2

Emotions and How We Handle Them

I don't know about you, but my heart is weary from the burden of my emotions. I am tired from always worrying about the next catastrophe to enter my life. I am worn from tears shed over unmet expectations, losses, and hurts. I am also frustrated with myself that time and again, I am host to emotions such as fear and despair. Is this just how life is? Should I just accept it? What do I do with all these emotions?

Emotions as we now know them have not always been this way. Emotions have not always held people captive. Emotions didn't always rule and enslave hearts and lives.

Before we continue in our journey to find the key of promise, we have to look back at how things were in the beginning.

The Origins of Despair

Since God is an emotional being, we know that emotions have always existed. God feels emotions such as love, joy, peace, jealousy, anger, and sadness (Exod. 34:14, Rom. 1:18, Rom. 5:5, John 11:35). In fact, it was out of His great love and joy that He created us. He desired to share with us the same perfect love that the Father, Son, and Holy Spirit have enjoyed together from all eternity.

We were created in the image of God and that means we feel things as well. This sets us apart from other creatures. It is part of what makes us human. When we feel love for our children, we are reflecting the love of our Creator. When we are angry at the evil in this world, we reflect the righteous anger of God. When we experience the joy of the Lord, we are reflecting the joy that the Trinity has always known and enjoyed within the Godhead.

So what happened? Why don't we experience emotions the way God intended them?

God did not create a world filled with shame and despair, fear or anxiety. In fact, when God voiced the world into existence, He declared that it was good. After creating humans, He declared that it was very good. The world at the beginning was perfect.

Adam and Eve are the only people in all of history who knew the world as sorrow-free, worry-free, and shame-free. Adam and Eve lived in perfect intimacy and harmony with one another. Scripture says that 'the man and his wife were both naked and were not ashamed' (Gen. 2:25). They enjoyed sweet fellowship with God, walking with Him in the cool of the evening. Their work was productive and fruitful. Nothing died or broke down; everything worked exactly as it should. There were no catastrophes around the corner, no safety violations to fret over, and no illnesses to catch. There weren't even any arguments, put-downs, or unmet expectations. Peace and joy reigned in their hearts.

Until the fateful day when Satan appeared in the Garden.

Disguised as a serpent, Satan appeared to Eve first and tempted her with the idea that she could be like God. Twisting truth, he encouraged her to try the forbidden fruit for herself.

> He said to the woman, 'Did God actually say, "You shall not eat of any tree in the garden?"' And the woman said to the serpent, 'We may eat of the fruit of the trees in the garden, but God said, "You shall not eat of the fruit of the tree that is in the midst of the garden, neither shall you touch it, lest you die."' But the serpent said to the woman, 'You will not surely die. For God knows that when you eat of it your eyes will be opened, and you will be like God, knowing good and evil' (Gen. 3:1-5).

She ate the fruit and passed it to Adam who did likewise. Sin then entered the world. The Bible says that the eyes of both were opened and they knew they were naked. Shame was birthed in their hearts. They tried to cover themselves and hide from God what they had done. God called out to them as He walked in the garden that evening. When He asked what they had done, the first round of 'The Blame Game' occurred right there on the forest floor. They threw each other under the proverbial bus and marital harmony was shattered.

He announced the curses due to them, mankind after them, and the physical world around them. But in grace, He promised a Savior, someone who would one day come and make all things right. 'I will put enmity between you and the woman, and between your offspring and her offspring: he shall bruise your head and you shall bruise his heel' (Gen. 3:15).

God then made the first animal sacrifice, clothing them with its skins, covering their sin and shame, a move that marked the beginning of sacrifice for sin that played over and over throughout the generations to come. Barred from the Garden, they left the perfect world they had known for a broken and fallen world they had brought into existence.

The intimate relationship Adam and Eve once enjoyed with God was broken. Their sin and the sin of every person born thereafter created a barrier between man and his Creator. The effects of sin only spread and spiraled from then on. Adam and Eve's son, Cain, killed his brother Abel in a jealous rage. The Old Testament recounts story after story of sorrow and heartache; of sin and shame; of war, death, and disease. Yet interwoven among all the sad stories is that crimson thread of the promised Savior who would one day come.

This is how we got to where we are. The fall explains why the world is the way it is. The heartache we experience, the loss, the fears, the rejection, all the pain we endure in this life is because of what happened that day back in Eden.

Sin is the cause of all our pain and sorrow. It might be the sins of others committed against us that bring us feelings of shame. It might be the effects of sin on the creation around us that bring a natural disaster, resulting in loss and our subsequent grief. It might be the brokenness of our bodies, causing us emotional turmoil or the failure of our minds to work as God intended. It might be our own sinful responses to what happens in our lives. It might even be a combination of all these, but at its root, sin is what brings us all our sorrows, griefs, and fears.

As we continue in this journey of exploring our emotions, let's take a look at how we often deal with our emotions. Not only did the painful emotions we experience not exist prior to the fall, but the way we respond to them and the way we handle them are also a result of the fall.

Fearing the Future
We were planning our first mission's trip as a family to Central America. As I planned and thought about the trip, my mind immediately thought about all the things that could go wrong. The town we were going to was two hours from the hospital. Our family has chronic illnesses. We've gone to the ER for stitches

and broken bones. I thought about all the risks for illnesses, potential broken bones, as well as all the accidents that could happen, and started feeling that sick feeling in my stomach.

I decided to make a list of all the things I should bring to prevent illnesses. I went to the pharmacy and bought out practically the entire store of over-the-counter medications. My mind continued to wander down meandering rabbit trails of the future, trying to anticipate all that could go wrong. I got myself so worked up that I started to dread our trip.

Fear. I was reacting out of fear. I had looked into my crystal ball and saw all the bad things that would happen and I wanted to be prepared for it. Wait a second. Back up. I don't have a crystal ball that shows the future and neither do you. But I like to think I do. In fact, fear tells me that I do. It tells me to prepare, plot, manage, anticipate, strategize, and predict. Like the man in Luke 12 who fills his storehouses for the future, I think that the more I prepare, the better I will be able to face what lies ahead. I then feel secure in my plans, trusting in my own success and strategic plans.

That is just one of the ways I try to manage my emotions. Let's explore several ways we might handle emotions: taking control, denial, and giving up.

Taking Control

Some of us try to handle our emotions, such as worry, fear, or anxiety by attempting to control all the things we worry or fear about. We make to-do lists and refuse to rest until each item is checked off. We research thoroughly everything that worries us. Google and Clorox are our two best friends. We disinfect throughout the day and keep our kids away from any child that seems to have the slightest runny nose.

Perhaps we find a solution to all our worries. We put all our hope in that basket and expect it to work. We trust in methods, solutions, and the latest research and live by them all. In effect, we worship our solutions. If a serious illness is what we fear, we'll put all our hope in special diets, medications, or exercise routines.

Control is something we all desire but none of us have. We don't know what will happen in the next moment, much less next year. Yet we still strive to take control of our lives. We make plans and pursue them. Scripture says that 'the heart of man plans his way, but the LORD establishes his steps' (Prov. 16:9).

Control was something Adam and Eve wanted. They desired to be like God, knowing good and evil. They wanted the sovereign control and knowledge that God has. As children of Adam, we desire the same. Our desire and pursuit of control are in fact a denial of God's control. We don't trust that His plans are good enough. We think we know better what we need. All the worrying, fretting, and stressing we do over our life situations stem from a lack of trust in God's good and perfect plan for us.

Psalm 112:7 says, 'He is not afraid of bad news; his heart is firm, trusting in the LORD.' Can you imagine having a heart that is firm, trusting in the Lord? This is the journey we are on, one that leads from worry to trust, from fear to dependence. If taking control is one of the ways you handle your emotions, seek God in repentance. In later chapters we will look at ways to face our worries and fears out of trust rather than control.

Denial

'I saw those new house decorations you bought. Why did you get those?' he asked.

'I thought they would look nice on the wall,' I said.

'Try not to spend too much on things like that. We really don't have the money.'

'I'm sorry,' I sighed. 'I think I've actually been lonely with you gone at work so much. Shopping gave me something to do.'

This conversation happened over a decade ago but I still remember it. That's because it was the first time I realized and connected my shopping habits with my loneliness. I finally came face to face with the fact that I used shopping in an attempt to fill a void in my heart.

I've since discovered other behaviors and practices in my life that I do to cover up uncomfortable feelings, losses, fears, worries, boredom, and stress. They are temporary distractions, ways to hide myself from the painful realities of life. For example, I remember being so tired and stressed from early motherhood that I literally said to myself, 'I deserve a diet soda today. I need a soda or I won't make it to bed time.' (I've said the same about chocolate!)

I also found myself longing for and looking for those rare moments of 'me time' at the end of the day. Whenever that time was interrupted, I reacted in frustration. That 'me time' had become my 'savior'.

We all have those things in our life that we use to hide our pain or to cover up things we'd rather not face. Shopping, eating, watching TV, playing on our phones, completing to-do lists, and keeping busy are all common ones. But ultimately, anything can become our 'savior,' something we look to in the hope that it will make our life better, easier, comfortable, and safe.

Pretending that we aren't feeling a particular emotion doesn't work for long. Eventually our emotions seep out in our actions and responses. The things we've filled our heart with show their worthlessness. We stand there empty with nothing left to hide behind. The reality is, we can't wish away our emotions. They always catch up to us.

Is denial or distraction a primary way you handle your emotions?

Giving Up and Giving In

Other times, we simply give up and let our emotions rule our lives. 'That's just the way I've always been,' we tell ourselves. We settle in to our despair or anger and just accept that they will always be with us. We make plans for the future with them, perhaps building them a room of their own.

Sometimes we may hide away from the world. We're better off alone, we think. We're safer away from the dangers and hurts of this world. So we withdraw from life and relationships. We keep away from anything that causes us fear or worry. Risk is a dirty word, and caution is the name of the game.

Never once do we consider standing up and fighting against them. That would be too much. So instead, we go through life always on alert for chaos and heartache. We live with the burden of despair permanently attached to our shoulders.

Yet the more we give up and allow our emotions to rule our lives, the more isolated and alone we become. After all, how can any of our friends fit into our living room, what with Worry, Despair, or Fear taking up all the space? The more we give in to our emotions, the more they rule us. Our lives become consumed with them.

But deep down, we know that's not how God wants us to live. After all, Jesus said He came to set us free. If you have been prone to giving in to your emotions, will you consider standing with me in resistance?

As we've explored some of the ways we handle our emotions, perhaps some of them resonated with you. You have to admit, they obviously don't work. They haven't freed us from our prisons. No amount of control actually changes anything, does it? Denial is just a way to live in an imaginary world. And giving in only ensures our imprisonment. But what if there is another way?

Remember the promised Savior, that seed God promised back in Genesis 3:15? Let's talk about Him next.

For Your Heart

1. What are some ways you have tried to manage your emotions?

2. Read the following passages: Matthew 11:29-30, Psalm 55:22, 1 Peter 5:7. What does Scripture say we should do with our burdens and cares?

3. Pray a prayer of repentance for the ways in which you have sinned with your emotions. Ask God to draw you to Himself and take your burdens from you.

3

Emotions Redeemed

Have you ever cleaned your house from top to bottom in one day? Or maybe spent a weekend getting your garage or basement completely cleaned and organized? It's such a great feeling to have everything clean at once. You run your finger over the bookshelves and it comes away without a speck of dust on it. You look at the neatly stacked boxes on the shelves in the garage and feel satisfied at the result of your hard work.

I remember one morning walking into the great room in my house just as the sun was rising. Its light was shining across the water in the pool at the back of the house. I stood transfixed, watching the sun's rays dance across the top of the pool. As I continued to watch, the sun rose a bit higher and the light stepped over the pool and pointed its rays through the sliding glass doors of the great room. Light began to shine on the kitchen countertop and in the stream of light I could see dust and grime everywhere. It woke me out of my sun-drunk trance and I realized my kitchen was not as clean as I thought it was. Though I had scrubbed it all down the night before, dirt still remained.

That's what light does; it reveals what's hidden in the darkness. The truth is, no matter how well everything is cleaned, it's not truly clean. Just look under the couch or behind the big television console and you'll find more dust and dirt than you can imagine. Once, we had to move the stove away from the wall because we had dropped a little knife in that small space between the counter and the stove. My husband and I both said, 'Ew! Yuck!' the moment we moved the stove. Ten years is a long time for dirt and grime to congregate together under a stove. And to be honest, I haven't wanted to move the stove again since.

Our Greatest Problem

This is especially true in our hearts. We can focus our time and energy cleaning ourselves up on the outside. We can work on changing our outward behaviors, trying to get them squeaky clean. We can read our Bible every day. We can faithfully serve in ministry. We can eat the right foods, provide the best education for our children, spend our money wisely, and watch the right channels on TV. We can do all the right things and yet behind all those actions, deep in the dark recesses of our heart, sin remains.

That's because our greatest problem isn't so much what can be seen on the outside. Our greatest problem is not our circumstances or the environment we live in. It's not that we need a vacation or that our kids are struggling in school. It's not that we need a better job or a bigger house.

Our greatest problem also is not that our dreams haven't come true or even that our closest friend hurt us. It's not that the doctor wants to run more tests or that our marriage is failing. It's not that our heart hurts from past memories, we suffer from paralyzing fears, or that we live with dark secrets of past shame. Our greatest problem is not any of those things.

Our greatest problem is sin. It's not only our greatest problem, but the greatest problem of everyone who has ever lived.

In the last chapter, we looked at the fall and how we got to this place of brokenness. Our world is broken. We are broken. Everyone around us is broken. 'As it is written: "None is righteous, no, not one"' (Rom. 3:10). Because of that first sin in the Garden, we are all born sinners. 'Behold, I was brought forth in iniquity, and in sin did my mother conceive me' (Ps. 51:5). Not only do we commit sins, we *are* sinners. Sin has infected every part of our being so much so that even our good works are like filthy rags in the sight of God (Isa. 64:6).

Not only is sin our greatest problem, but it also has a great consequence. Scripture tells us, 'For the wages of sin is death, but the free gift of God is eternal life in Christ Jesus our Lord' (Rom. 6:23). Question 19 of the *Westminster Shorter Catechism* sums it up like this:

> Q. 19. What is the misery of that estate where into man fell?
>
> A. All mankind by their fall lost communion with God, are under his wrath and curse, and so made liable to all miseries in this life, to death itself, and to the pains of hell forever.

Our greatest problem is not something that we can fix. There is no ten-step solution or self-help book that is going to cure us. No matter how hard we try to change our lives, our circumstances, or other people, the problem of sin will always get in the way. There is nothing we can do to rescue ourselves from the curse of death and eternal separation from God.

Paul Tripp describes our greatest problem like this:

> It is the evil that is inside of you that either magnetizes you to the evil outside of you or causes you to deal with the evil outside of you in a way that is wrong. It is only when you begin to accept that your greatest problem in all of life is not what has happened or been done to you that you begin

to get excited about the rescuing grace of Jesus Christ. It is only when you begin to accept that your greatest need is something with which you came into the world that you will begin to hunger for the help that only God can give you. It is only then that you will begin to hunger for more than change of situation and relationship. It is only then that you will begin to accept the most radical and personally liberating truth that you could ever conceive. What is that truth? It is that what you and I really need to be rescued from is ourselves! We are the biggest danger to ourselves. That is why God offers us the gorgeous promise of his grace which has the power to change us from the inside out.[1]

A Great Solution
As God promised in Genesis 3:15, we need a Savior. We need someone who can step in and redeem us. We need someone who can pay the hostage taker so we can be released from our prison. We need a Rescuer who can set us free from our captivity to sin.

In the Old Testament times, most people were farmers. They tilled the soil and grew crops to provide the food they needed to live. Sometimes things happened in their life to the point where they became poor and had to sell their land to pay their debts. If they had a relative who was financially able, their relative would step in as their redeemer and buy their land back for them, settling their debts and allowing them to return home.

---

1. Tripp, Paul. *Whiter Than Snow: Meditations on Sin and Mercy* (Chicago: Crossway, 2008), p. 39.

Like those farmers, we were in deep debt. Yet the debt we owed was huge—eternal death and separation from God. God is holy and nothing can be in His presence that is not holy. That is why Adam and Eve had to leave the Garden. It's why the Israelites could not even touch Mt. Sinai or they would die. It's why Moses had to take off his sandals when he stood before the Lord. It's why we needed a Redeemer to pay our debt for us.

Until that Redeemer came, payment had to be made to atone for sin and that payment was in the form of a sacrifice. A lamb or goat was offered in the place of a person's life. It was insufficient and temporary; that sacrifice had to be repeated day in and day out for centuries.

That's why Jesus stepped in and settled our debt before God. Christ entered the story of redemption Himself. He wrapped Himself in human flesh and lived in this sin-stained world, experiencing every heartache and temptation we face. He knew poverty, sickness, hunger, homelessness, injustice, rejection, grief, and everything that we experience as humans in this fallen world. Yet He never sinned once. Because of His perfect life, He was able to be the perfect sacrifice. He took our place at the cross, suffered for us, and endured the separation from His Father that was ours, took on the wrath of God, bore our sins, and died the death that we deserved. 'Christ redeemed us from the curse of the law by becoming a curse for us—for it is written, "Cursed is everyone who is hanged on a tree"' (Gal. 3:13).

Because He was sinless, the grave could not keep Him. He rose from the dead three days later in victory. Through the gift of faith in what He accomplished for us, we have been redeemed. We have been restored into right relationship with our Maker and Creator. When God looks at us, He sees the perfect righteousness of Christ and not our sin. We can now come into His presence with confidence. We have been adopted into the family of God and have the hope of eternity with Him forever.

Our Greatest Need

But Christ didn't just come to rescue us from sin; He came to restore us back to God. He came to give us what we needed most—God Himself. We were made to be in community with God. We were made to love, worship, and adore Him. We were made to experience that perfect love, joy, and unity that the Triune Godhead has experienced from before time began. We were made to know Him and be known by Him.

Apart from Christ, we wander the world aimless, always searching and pursuing what our heart needs most but never finding it. We seek after false loves and counterfeit solutions but nothing quite fits that God-shaped hole in our heart.

Jesus came to restore that intimate union that Adam and Eve had with God before the fall. Sometimes when we think of what Jesus did for us, we only think of our salvation in terms of forgiveness and getting a spot reserved for us in heaven. But that is only like looking at part of a picture. It is incomplete.

In his book, *God Is the Gospel: Meditations on God's Love as the Gift of Himself*, John Piper asks this sobering question: 'The critical question for our generation – and for every generation – is this: If you could have heaven, with no sickness, and with all the friends you ever had on earth, and all the food you ever liked, and all the leisure activities you ever enjoyed, and all the natural beauties you ever saw, all the physical pleasures you ever tasted, and no human conflict or any natural disasters, could you be satisfied with heaven, if Christ were not there?'[2]

This question gets at the heart of what we believe about who God is and why Christ came. It points out that we can view Christ's death and the salvation He purchased as an insurance policy that provides for our place in heaven. God then becomes our cosmic candy dispenser, granting our whims at the push of a prayer. If we desire all the comforts and joys of heaven and could not care less if Christ was not there, then we have missed the point of Christ's death for us entirely.

John Piper continues, 'Christ did not die to forgive sinners who go on treasuring anything above seeing and savoring God. And people who would be happy in heaven if Christ were not there, will not be there. The gospel is not a way to get people to heaven; it is a way to get people to God. It's a way of overcoming every obstacle to everlasting joy in God. If we don't want God above all things, we have not been converted by the gospel.'[3]

2.　　Piper, John. *God is the Gospel: Meditations on God's Love as the Gift of Himself* (Chicago: Crossway, 2005), p. 15.

3.　　Ibid., p. 47.

This question that John Piper asks is convicting. It reveals that my own heart often wants the good things God gives more than God Himself. I care more about that spot on the bus to heaven than I do about Who I am going to see when I get there. I want all of God's blessings, promises, and answered prayers more than I want God Himself. This is proven by the way I react when I don't get what I want. When my dreams don't come true or my child gets sick or a job is lost or I don't get the house I always wanted or relationships fail or leaders in my church let me down or the depression doesn't lift—how I respond shows more of what I think of Christ and His place of importance in my heart.

It is important that we understand that our greatest need is God Himself. Our greatest need is to be in communion with Him. Our sin is what separated us from Him and Christ's redemption did away with that separation. The purpose of His death was to reunite us with our first love.

The problem is that we can often forget this. Instead of seeking after God, we seek and pursue joy in all the wrong places. What we think we need most is often far from the truth. Real joy and happiness do not come through things, relationships, carefree days, obedient children, blissful marriages, good jobs, healthy bodies, and comfortable lives. It comes from being in right relationship with God. Jesus came to restore that relationship and reverse what happened in the Garden and He did so through His blood shed on the cross. He didn't die to make our lives comfortable or to be our wish granter. He came to bring us the joy of knowing God and being known by God.

The amazing grace of the gospel is that it covers even our forgetfulness. Even when we wander far from our first love, God's grace always draws us back. Even when we forget and fail Him, He never fails us. His love for us is greater than our worst sin.

When we get distracted by the things of this world and begin to desire the things that God gives more than God Himself, we can turn again to the cross of Jesus and find the forgiveness we desperately need. In fact, as we'll look at later, returning to the gospel is something we need to do each and every day.

A Savior Who Redeems All Things ... Including Our Emotions

You may wonder, why all this talk about sin, Jesus, and the cross? For some of you, it may be familiar territory and ground you've covered long ago. You might be thinking, 'I thought this was a book about the Psalms.' And you are right. It is. But since all of Scripture is about Jesus, so is this book. Since all of Scripture points to Christ, our need for Him, and what He has done for us, the good news of the gospel is central to what we will talk about in this book. In fact, it is the common thread running through every page.

(Before we get too far, I should tell you that when I use the term *gospel*, I am referring to the complete work of Christ in His life, death, and resurrection for us, as well as His current and ongoing work in us through His Spirit.)

So how does reviewing the gospel help us with our emotions?

Jesus came to redeem all things—including our emotions. He not only set us free from sin, provided our forever forgiveness, and restored us back to the joy of knowing God, but He also set us free from all things that hold us captive. For those of us who are held captive by our emotions, this is good news indeed! Jesus Himself said, 'The Spirit of the Lord is upon me, because he has anointed me to proclaim good news to the poor. He has sent me to proclaim liberty to the captives and recovering of sight to the blind, to set at liberty those who are oppressed,' (Luke 4:18). In Romans, Paul wrote, 'For the law of the Spirit of life has set you free in Christ Jesus from the law of sin and death' (8:2). 'For sin will have no dominion over you, since you are not under law but under grace' (Rom. 6:14).

We are no longer slaves to sin, but instead are slaves to righteousness. 'Likewise, my brothers, you also have died to the law through the body of Christ, so that you may belong to another, to him who has been raised from the dead, in order that we may bear fruit for God' (Rom. 7:4). 'But now that you have been set free from sin and have become slaves of God, the fruit you get leads to sanctification and its end, eternal life' (Rom. 6:22). If we are in Christ, we've been given His Spirit who lives in us. We live under His influence and power. He lives and reigns in our hearts, compelling us to love and obey God.

As the first question of the *Heidelberg Catechism* puts it:

Q. What is your only comfort in life and death?

A. That I am not my own, but belong with body and soul, both in life and in death, to my faithful Savior Jesus Christ. He has fully paid for all my sins with his precious blood, and has set me free from all the power of the devil. He also preserves me in such a way that without the will of my heavenly Father not a hair can fall from my head; indeed, all things must work together for my salvation. Therefore, by his Holy Spirit he also assures me of eternal life and makes me heartily willing and ready from now on to live for him.

Though we have been freed from sin's power, the presence of sin still remains. We still live in a sinful world. People will still hurt us. Tragedies will continue to happen. We still have sin that lingers within us. As Jerry Bridges wrote, 'Even though our hearts have been renewed, even though we have been freed from the absolute dominion of sin, even though God's Holy Spirit dwells within our bodies, this principle of sin still lurks within us and wages war against our souls.'[4]

During our days here on earth, God, through His Spirit, is stripping us of that sin. He is refining us, changing us, and transforming us into the likeness of Christ. He is making us into who we already are in Christ.

The Spirit convicts us through the Word of God. He prompts our hearts when we've strayed. He helps us to resist temptation. He protects us from evil. He comforts us in our sorrows. He points us to the truth. And through His work in us, He bears in us fruit of

---

4.   Bridges, Jerry. *Respectable Sins: Confronting the Sins We Tolerate* (Colorado Springs: NavPress, 2007), p. 24.

righteousness. 'But the fruit of the Spirit is love, joy, peace, patience, kindness, goodness, faithfulness, gentleness, self-control ...' (Gal. 5:22-23).

We Need the Gospel Every Day

We need these truths of the gospel every day. We need to remember the depths of our sin. We need to remember our great need for a Savior. We need to remember that it is out of God's great grace that He provided a way to bring us back to Himself. We need to remember all that Christ accomplished for us at the cross. For the gospel has power not only at the moment of our salvation, but in every moment of our lives.

The gospel of grace has not only saved us from our sins in the past and those in the future, but also empowers us in the present. It is applicable in our daily struggles of walking by faith. It frees us from the bondage of bitterness, anger, worry, fear, despair, and doubt. It comforts us as we remember that our Savior knows what it is like to live in a dark world where we are hurt, abandoned, and rejected. As we reflect on all that Christ did for us in His perfect life, sacrificial death, victorious resurrection, and His work in us through His Spirit, our strength is renewed.

When fatigue overwhelms us, we can remember the strength that is already in us by the power of the Holy Spirit. When we are frustrated with our children and we fail in our parenting, we can recall all that Christ did for us on the cross. He died for us, knowing we could not be a perfect parent. When we are hurt and angry by the way other people treat us, we can remember how we've been forgiven for much worse. When we are in despair about the trials in our lives or our heart aches from the evil inflicted on us by others, we can remember that the Man of Sorrows bore all our pain and will one day take away all our tears forever.

The truths of the gospel are for our every day. We must know these truths. They must saturate our heart. They must be the daily bread we feast on and the water of life that we drink.

When it comes to our journey through the laments, these truths are our foundational truths. They are like the passport you need to take with you when you travel. You can't enter a country without a passport. And you can't be found without one on your person. For us, the gospel must be with us in this journey through the laments. We can't be found without it. We must tuck it into our pocket like Christian in the story of *Pilgrim's Progress* and keep it with us on our journey. We'll explore some of those reasons why in the next chapter.

For Your Heart

1. Sometimes we think we've heard the gospel enough and that what we need is something new. Do you ever think that? Do you know that the gospel has provided for your greatest need?

2. What does it mean to you that Christ redeemed you and restored you back into fellowship with God?

3. What does it mean to you to know that Christ has set you free from your captivity and that you don't have to be controlled by your sin, your past, or even your emotions?

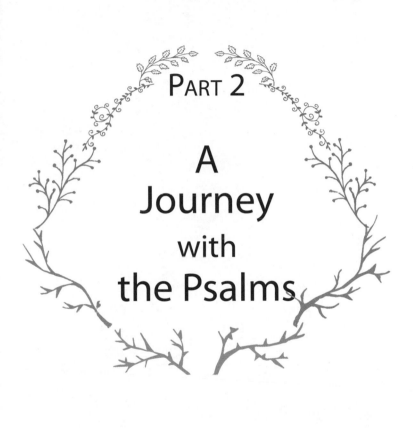

PART 2

A
Journey
with
the Psalms

4

Jesus and the Psalms

Have you ever gone on a trip, and when you arrived at your destination, realized that you had forgotten something important? It seems to be a regular habit of mine to forget to pack something necessary and vital. I've forgotten to pack my husband's glasses on more than one occasion. I have also forgotten cell phone chargers, medications, and most recently, a booster seat. We end up using valuable time and money going to the store and replacing the forgotten items. It gets us off track and delays our journey.

When it comes to our journey with the psalmist, before we move into the laments, bringing our emotions with us, we don't want to get too far without being adequately prepared. Like any journey we travel, we want to be prepared, knowing where we are going and having what we need with us. So before we look at the Psalms of Lament in particular, we want to look at the book of Psalms and understand its place in the context of the big picture of Scripture.

The Psalms are part of the genre of wisdom literature. If you spent any time in Sunday School as a child, you quickly learned to find the Psalms smack dab in the middle of our Bibles, situated alongside the other wisdom books of Job, Proverbs, Ecclesiastes, and Song of Solomon. The Psalms are a collection of poems, written by a variety of authors including Moses, David, Solomon, the sons of Korah, among others. Besides the laments, there are also psalms of thanksgiving, praise, confidence, confession, and remembrance. The book of Psalms was used in Hebrew worship and sung to God in the same way we sing hymns in church on Sunday morning.

The Psalms Whisper Jesus' Name
While it's easy to read a psalm and immediately apply it to our struggles in our daily life, we also have to take into account the way the psalm fits into the greater story God has written. The Bible isn't

a series of disjointed books that have nothing to do with one another. Rather, the Bible is one big story about God's redemption of His people through His Son, Jesus.

Jesus is the big picture. The Bible is about Him. The Old Testament points forward to Him and the New Testament points back to Him. Jesus is the One promised in Genesis 3:15, 'I will put enmity between you and the woman, and between your offspring and her offspring; he shall bruise your head, and you shall bruise his heel.' He is the One that Moses spoke of when he said, 'The LORD your God will raise up for you a prophet like me from among you, from your brothers—it is to him you shall listen' (Deut. 18:15). He is the One the Israelites waited for and the One the prophets promised would come. As the subtitle of the *Jesus Storybook Bible* says, 'every story whispers his name.'

This is what Jesus Himself attested. After Jesus rose from the dead, He met a couple of disciples on the road to Emmaus. They didn't realize at first that it was Him. Thinking He was a stranger who didn't know all that had happened, they explained to Him about Jesus and His crucifixion saying, 'But we had hoped that he was the one to redeem Israel' (Luke 24:21). And Jesus said to them, '"O foolish ones, and slow of heart to believe all that the prophets have spoken! Was it not necessary that the Christ should suffer these things and enter into his glory?" And beginning with Moses and all the Prophets, he interpreted to them in all the Scriptures the things concerning himself' (Luke 24:25-27). Later, when

Jesus appeared in a home where these disciples had gathered with others, He said to them, '"These are my words that I spoke to you while I was still with you, that everything written about me in the Law of Moses and the Prophets and the Psalms must be fulfilled"' (Luke 24:44).

Jesus Himself said that the book of Psalms was ultimately about Him. To read the Psalms without that understanding is to read them contrary to how Jesus told us to read them. As the *Gospel Transformation Bible* puts it, we need to understand that the book of Psalms 'plays a contributing role in the history of redemption that culminates in Jesus. The Bible is in essence a message of what God has done to redeem and restore sinners, and this is done preeminently in the person and work of Christ. Each book of the Bible carries forward the supreme redemptive purpose, a purpose that comes to a decisive climax in Jesus.'[1]

The book of Psalms contains the heart cries of God's covenant people. As Christians, as believers in Jesus Christ, the promised Messiah who came to deliver His people from sin, we know that Christ fulfilled all the heart cries of God's people. The *Gospel Transformation Bible* says it best, 'Jesus is God's definitive answer to the cries of his people.'[2]

The New Testament and the Psalms

Reading the Psalms through a Christ-centered lens is not just some trendy way to read the Bible. It's the way the New Testament writers viewed the Psalms.

---

1.   *Gospel Transformation Bible* (Chicago: Crossway, 2013), p. 653.

2.   Ibid., p. 654.

In fact, the Psalms are referenced more than any other book in the New Testament. Paul quotes the Psalms often in his letters. Sometimes he quotes the Psalms in order to teach truths about Jesus, and other times it is to teach specific doctrines. For example, in Romans 3, Paul refers to several different psalms when he discusses the doctrine of total depravity. Quoting Psalm 14, he says, 'No one does good, not even one' (Rom. 3:12). And in Acts 13:33, Paul quotes Psalm 2:7 and applies it specifically to Jesus, 'You are my Son; today I have begotten you.' Paul, like the other New Testament writers, 'read the Psalms from a Christian perspective and saw Jesus.'[3]

In another example, Peter, preaching to the crowd in Acts 2, quoted David in Psalm 16 and applied it to Jesus. Speaking about Jesus' death and resurrection, Peter said, 'For David says concerning him, "I saw the Lord always before me, for he is at my right hand that I may not be shaken; therefore my heart was glad and my tongue rejoiced; my flesh also will dwell in hope. For you will not abandon my soul to Hades, or let your Holy One see corruption. You have made known to me the paths of life; you will make me full of gladness with your presence"' (Acts 2:25-28).

Paul also preached on this same passage when he was in Pisidian Antioch in Acts 13. To the Jews gathered there and the God-fearing Gentiles, Paul quoted Psalm 16:10, '"You will not let your Holy

---

3.   Longman, Tremper III. *How to Read the Psalms* (Downers Grove, IL: InterVarsity Press, 1988), p. 66.

One see corruption." For David, after he had served the purpose of God in his own generation, fell asleep and was laid with his fathers and saw corruption, but he whom God raised up did not see corruption.' (Acts 13:35-37). Paul here asserts that Psalm 16 can't be ultimately about David because David was dead and buried. It was Jesus who fulfilled this verse when He rose from dead.

The Psalms, like the other Old Testament books, all look forward to Christ. However, they also have an immediate, here and now meaning for the author and original readers. These poems are heart cries of real people who went through real struggles and real trials. They were hurt and afraid. They felt abandoned, sorrowful, and angry. At the same time, the Psalms also have a deeper theme, that of Jesus Christ.

For example, in Psalm 16 which I mentioned above, David wrote it as a song of trust in the midst of an illness. He was sick, but trusted God that the illness would not kill him. However, as Acts 2 says, David knew that his psalm also pointed to the Messiah to come, 'Brothers, I may say to you with confidence about the patriarch David that he both died and was buried, and his tomb is with us to this day. Being therefore a prophet, and knowing that God had sworn with an oath to him that he would set one of his descendants on his throne, he foresaw and spoke about the resurrection of the Christ, that he was not abandoned to Hades, nor did his flesh see corruption.' (vv. 29-31). As Christians, we can read this psalm and see Jesus. We can also see that the psalm applies to our own lives. We know that because of Jesus' resurrection, we have a confident hope in eternity. Because of Jesus, we know even more than those in the Old Testament did what happens to us after we die.[4] Therefore, as we read the Psalms, we need to remember the redemptive purpose and Christ's fulfillment of the psalm while at the same time also applying the psalm to our own life.

Now that we know that the Psalms, like all of Scripture, are Christ-centered and ultimately fulfilled in Him, how do we read the Psalms in light of that?

Words by Christ

In Colossians 3:16, Paul encourages us to let the Word of Christ dwell in us, by singing 'psalms, hymns, and spiritual songs.' 'Let the word of Christ dwell in you richly, teaching and admonishing one another in all wisdom, singing psalms and hymns and spiritual songs, with thankfulness in your hearts to God.' Mark Futato, in reference to this passage, says that the Greek words Paul uses for 'psalms, hymns, and spiritual songs' are all used in the Greek translation of the Old Testament. 'These three words are used in the titles to various psalms. So while "the word of Christ" includes more than the Psalms, the Psalms are "the word of Christ." "The word of Christ" here would mean "the word spoken about Christ" in the first place and "the word spoken by Christ" in the second place. When reading a psalm, it is helpful to read that psalm as speaking about Christ and to read it as being spoken by Christ.'[5] He goes on to say that

---

4.   Longman. *How to Read the Psalms*, p. 68.

5.   Futato, Mark D. *Joy Comes in the Morning: Psalms for all Seasons* (Phillipsburg, NJ: P&R Publishing, 2004), p. 14.

the Psalms of Lament in particular can be read as though they are being spoken by Christ. 'When we sing or read the laments, we are singing and reading about Christ, who has gone before us and sung the laments for us.'[6]

Hebrews 5:7 tells that Jesus did sing and pray the laments, 'In the days of his flesh, Jesus offered up prayers and supplications, with loud cries and tears, to him who was able to save him from death, and he was heard because of his reverence.' We remember Jesus' heart cries on the night of His betrayal, how He sweated drops of blood as He anticipated what was to come when He would lay down His life for His people. There on His knees in Gethsemane, Jesus voiced His own lament, 'Father, if you are willing, remove this cup from me. Nevertheless, not my will, but yours, be done' (Luke 22:42). From the cross, He quoted David's lament in Psalm 22:1, 'And at the ninth hour Jesus cried with a loud voice, "Eloi, Eloi, lema sabachthani?" which means, "My God, my God, why have you forsaken me?"' (Mark 15:34).

We know from the last chapter that Jesus knows what it is like to live in this sin-stained world. He endured the pain, sorrow, suffering, rejection, and temptation that we have endured, yet never sinned. 'For we do not have a high priest who is unable to sympathize with our weaknesses, but one who in every respect has been tempted as we are, yet without sin. Let us then with confidence draw near

---

6.   Futato, Mark D. *Joy Comes in the Morning: Psalms for all Seasons*, p. 14.

to the throne of grace, that we may receive mercy and find grace to help in time of need' (Heb. 4:15-16). It is because of Jesus and through Jesus that we can come before the Father in confidence and pour out our hearts at His feet.

When we open the book of Psalms, we must remember its place in the context of the story of redemption. We can't read them apart from Christ. The laments in particular remind us that Jesus walked the journey of the laments before us. When we read the words of David, we can remember Jesus, 'How long must I take counsel in my soul and have sorrow in my heart all the day? How long shall my enemy be exalted over me?' (Ps. 13:2). We can remember that He was the Man of Sorrows, familiar with suffering. We can remember that He was despised and rejected. We can remember our Savior, who lived a life of sorrow and suffering for us so that we could be freed forever from the curse of sin.

Songs to Our Savior

In addition to reading the Psalms of Lament as the words spoken by Christ, we can read them and use them in our own songs and prayers to Christ. We can claim the words of the laments as our own and cry out to Christ, just as the psalmist cried out to God.

This is because Jesus is God the Son, the second person of the Trinity. He was there at the beginning. 'He is the image of the invisible God, the firstborn of all creation. For by him all things were created, in heaven and on earth, visible and invisible, whether thrones or dominions or rulers or authorities—all things were created through him and for him. And he is before all things, and in him all things hold together. And he is the head of the body, the church. He is the beginning, the firstborn from the dead, that in everything he might be preeminent. For in him all the fullness of God was pleased to dwell, and through him to reconcile to himself all things, whether on earth or in heaven, making peace by the blood of his cross.' (Col. 1:15-20). While during the Old Testament era, the Psalms were sung to Yahweh, God the Father, it is appropriate for us as Christians to sing and pray these Psalms to Jesus the Son.[7]

As we journey into the Psalms of Lament together, expressing our own sorrows and fears to God, we will be looking at the Psalms in the way I've discussed in this chapter. We will claim them as our own and use them to cry out to Christ for help and we will look to see how Christ fulfilled the psalm and our heart's cries at the cross.

For Your Heart

1. What does it mean to you that Jesus has fulfilled the heart's cries of His people at the cross?

2. Can you see how every story, including the Psalms, whispers His name?

3. Read Psalm 27. Take some time to consider how you can relate to the psalm. Then meditate on how Christ has fulfilled the psalm.

---

7.   Longman. *How to Read the Psalms*, p. 69.

5

The Psalms of Lament

In the first chapter, we looked at how emotions can hold us captive, how they often reign and rule our hearts, and also explored some of those emotions in detail. I promised you a journey to seek freedom from being led by your emotions and that journey continues in this chapter as we begin to get into the Psalms of Lament.

The Lost Art of Lament

There is a science show I've seen on television that focuses on new discoveries scientists have made about the brain. In one particular episode, they talked about a patch that was being developed to help people who were grieving the loss of a loved one. The patch is designed to help the person go through the stages of grief quickly, so they can get it over with in a shorter amount of time.

Like all things in life, we tend to want to push through the difficult and hard things. If possible, we'd like to avoid pain altogether. When it comes to emotional pain and turmoil, we tend to avoid painful feelings rather than face them. As we explored in Chapter 2, we'd rather mask them, ignore them, deny them, or minimize them. We keep ourselves busy so we don't have to think about how hard life really is. We distract ourselves from pain through food, shopping, sex, alcohol, and entertainment. We don't know how to hurt, to grieve, or to experience heartache.

In Western culture, we have lost the art of lament. For those in Old Testament times, expressing one's grief and sorrow was the expected way to go through the hard times of life. The Israelites were always speaking to God with honesty and raw emotion. They bombarded Him with questions and expected Him to respond. They cried out to Him in the face of all their fears, sorrows, and shame.

Sometimes we can feel uncomfortable with the laments in Scripture. They are too honest and real. They ask questions of God that we can't imagine having the nerve to ask. The level of passion and assertiveness that the laments express seems to cross some line that we fear to cross.

Author Paul Miller, in *A Loving Life: In a World of Broken Relationships*, discusses the honesty of the laments:

> Such honesty seldom characterizes our praying. Our inability to lament is primarily due to the influence of the Greek mind on the early church. Greek Stoicism believed that emotions—anything that interrupted the goal of a calm and balanced life—were bad. The passionate person was the immature person. Balance was everything ... A lament grieves that the world is unbalanced. It grieves at the gap between reality and God's promise. It believes in a God who is there, who can act in time and place. It doesn't drift into cynicism or unbelief, but engages God passionately with what's wrong.[1]

This world is a sinful, broken place. Things are not as they should be. Loved ones die, people hurt and reject us, and temptations surround us on every side. We need to be honest about the horrors and sorrows of this world. We need to cry out to God for help. We need to come to the One who is sovereign over all things and lay our cares at His feet.

We need to be believers who know how to lament, not simply for the sake of catharsis or emotional relief, but because we believe that God

---

1.   Miller, Paul. *A Loving Life: In a World of Broken Relationships* (Chicago, IL: Crossway, 2014), Kindle Edition, Location: 414.

rules and reigns over all things. We need to lament not because we are without hope but because we have faith in God. We also need to lament so that we can enter into the pain we so often avoid in order to know the peace that God gives those who come to Him in faith. We need to lament so that we can learn more about God, about His redemptive purposes in this world, about ourselves, and about our greatest need in Christ. And we need to lament so that we can experience more of God's amazing grace.

Why the Psalms of Lament?

It was God's Word that started this blue marble spinning in the Milky Way. It was His Word that created mankind and said, 'It is very good.' It was His Word that opened the sea to let the Israelites cross over into freedom and it was His Word at the cross that declared redemption accomplished when Christ cried out, 'It is finished!'

The Bible is God's written Word. It is God breathed, 'All Scripture is breathed out by God' (2 Tim. 3:16). It is also our final rule and authority. Everything else in this world has to stand up to its light. Only the Bible contains God's Word and by its light, we view everything else.

God's Word is what sanctifies us, changes, and transforms us. Jesus prayed for the disciples, 'Sanctify them in the truth; your word is truth' (John 17:17). Hebrews tells us that, 'the word of God is living and active, sharper than any two-edged sword, piercing to the division of soul and of spirit, of joints and of marrow, and discerning the thoughts and intentions of the heart' (4:12).

When it comes to understanding our emotions and knowing how to express them, God's Word is our authority there as well. In His grace, He has given us the Psalms of Lament to help us navigate the painful emotions and circumstances of life. In reading and studying the laments, we will be changed by them. They will give us hope. They will draw us deeper into His grace.

The laments will:

1. *Help us to express our feelings*: We will learn that God desires that we come to Him with all our sorrows. The laments will teach us just how to express our feelings to God. We'll learn to be real and honest before Him. They will give us the words we need to express the deepest groanings of our heart.

2. *Shape our feelings*: Not only will we learn how to come to God with our emotions, we will also find that the laments will help us take that raw emotion and shape it for God's glory. 'The Psalms do not simply express emotions: when sung in faith, they actually shape the emotions of the godly. The emotions are therefore not a problem to be solved but are part of the raw material of now-fallen humanity that can be shaped to good and noble ends. The Psalms, as songs, act deeply on the emotions, for the good of God's people. It is not "natural" to trust God in hardship, and yet the Psalms provide a way of doing just that, and enable the singers to trust better as a result of singing them.'[2]

---

2. *ESV Study Bible* (Chicago: Crossway, 2008), Kindle Edition, Location: 122113.

3. *Teach us more about ourselves*: As we read the laments we will undoubtedly learn more about ourselves. We'll see ways in which we have tried to deny our feelings. We'll see the ways we have trusted in false substitutes and counterfeit loves to meet the needs that only God can meet. We'll see how we have trusted in our own strength rather than God's. We'll also see sins for which we need to repent.

As the authors of *The Cry of the Soul: How Our Emotions Reveal Our Deepest Questions About God* put it: 'The psalmist's ruthless honesty compels us to look beyond the surface of our tumult, deeper into our soul, where we expose our battle with God. As the psalmist cries "out of the depths" (Ps. 130:1), we find ourselves crying out to God along with him. The Psalms disrupt our assumptions that we can escape the "groaning" of this life. They call us back from our natural tendency to flee from pain and fight against any who provoke discomfort. They expose the essence of our emotional turmoil — the commitment to find life apart from trusting God.'[3]

4. *Teach us more about God*: The laments will teach us more about God. They will point us to His character, His goodness, His faithfulness, and His grace. They will show us that He alone is our refuge and salvation.

5. *Reorient us to the Truth*: The laments will point us away from ourselves and our circumstances and to

---

3.   Allender, Dan B. and Longman, Tremper, III. *The Cry of the Soul: How Our Emotions Reveal Our Deepest Questions About God* (Colorado Springs: NavPress, 1994), Kindle Edition, Location: 235.

the One who alone can help us. They will help us to identify lies we have believed and will reorient our hearts to the truth in God's Word. They will show us that the source of all our hope and peace is found in Christ alone.

Let's now look at the laments, their place in the book of Psalms and some of their defining characteristics.

The Psalms as a Songbook

When I was in high school, I transferred from a public school to a Christian school. The administration of the school were strict psalmists, meaning they believed in singing only the Psalms in worship. In my church, I was used to singing either from the hymnbook with pianist accompaniment or singing praise songs led by the worship band. So it was an eye-opening experience for me to sing from the Psalter every school morning.

The Psalter is a book that has two sets of pages, the words of the Psalms to be sung and the musical tunes to use in singing the Psalms. Each morning our classroom teacher would tell us what psalm we were singing and then what tune we were singing it to. To this day, many years later, I can still hum the tune we always sang to Psalm 23.

As strange as it seemed to me to sing the Psalms, the Psalms were the songbook for the Israelites. And just like today where we have different songs to reflect the mood and life circumstance we are in, so too did the Israelites have songs to sing depending on what was going on in their lives. Think of the songs we sing at a sporting event. We don't sing the blues or a love song, we sing songs that rally everyone together to cheer and root for their team. Likewise, at a wedding reception, we dance to songs about forever love, not morose songs about a recent breakup. For the Israelites, they had songs to sing when they were sad as well as when they were joyful; songs for when they were repentant and for when they were fearful. As the *ESV Study Bible* puts it, 'The Psalter is the songbook of the people of God in their gathered worship. These songs cover a wide range of experiences and emotions, and give God's people the words to express these emotions and to bring these experiences before God.'[4]

Genre in the Psalms

The book of Psalms contains different genres or types of psalms. A genre 'refers to a group of texts similar in their mood, content, structure, or phraseology.'[5] Scholars have grouped like psalms together into a variety of genres, and unfortunately, like many other things in Scripture, scholars disagree over how many different genres there are. For the sake of simplicity, I will describe the main ones.

For the Israelites, when God had moved in an amazing way, rescuing them from their enemies, they sang psalms of Thanksgiving. 'Oh give thanks to the LORD, for he is good; his love endures forever' (Ps. 118:29). When their enemies were hunting them down, they sang laments. 'O LORD, how many are

---

4. Allender and Longman. *The Cry of the Soul: How Our Emotions Reveal Our Deepest Questions About God* , Location: 122107.

5. Longman. *How to Read the Psalms*, p. 21.

my foes!' (Ps. 3:1a). When they wanted to dwell on God's past deliverance on their behalf, they sang songs of remembrance. 'He divided the sea and led them through it, and made the water stand up like a heap. In the daytime he led them with a cloud, and all the night with a fiery light' (Ps. 78:13-14). Other genres include songs of praise, songs of wisdom, songs of confession, songs of confidence, and songs of kingship or royalty.

Laments in the Bible
While all the genres of the Psalms are important for us to read, pray through, and sing, for the purposes of this book, we are only going to focus on the laments. The Psalms are not the only place where we find laments, for the Bible is filled with them. The book of Isaiah contains laments over the prophesied punishments God would pour out over the nations. 'Therefore I weep with the weeping of Jazer for the vine of Sibmah; I drench you with my tears, O Heshbon and Elealeh; for over your summer fruit and your harvest the shout has ceased. And joy and gladness are taken away from the fruitful field, and in the vineyards no songs are sung, no cheers are raised; no treader treads out wine in the presses; I have put an end to the shouting. Therefore my inner parts moan like a lyre for Moab, and my inmost self for Kir-hareseth' (Isa. 16:9-11).

The book of Lamentations is one very long lament written by the prophet Jeremiah. In Lamentations, Jeremiah guides the people in lamenting over what happened to the city of Jerusalem and the people of

God by the Babylonians. 'My eyes are spent with weeping; my stomach churns; my bile is poured out to the ground because of the destruction of the daughter of my people, because infants and babies faint in the streets of the city' (2:11).

In the book of Ruth, upon her return to Bethlehem, Naomi lamented the losses she had experienced, 'Do not call me Naomi; call me Mara, for the Almighty has dealt very bitterly with me. I went away full, and the Lord has brought me back empty. Why call me Naomi, when the Lord has testified against me and the Almighty has brought calamity upon me?' (1:20-21). Jesus Himself lamented the death of His friend Lazarus in John 11. Following the stoning of Stephen, the book of Acts tells us, 'Devout men buried Stephen and made great lamentation over him' (8:2).

Defining Characteristics of the Psalms of Lament

When it comes to the songs of lament in the book of Psalms, these are the songs sung to God when one's heart is weary, full, and sad. There are no cheerful show tunes or sports anthems here. They are the blues melodies of the Psalms. The tone is dark and bleak. These psalms take place in the deep pits of sorrow into which the storms of life toss us. They express all the difficult and hard feelings of life such as grief, anger, abandonment, loneliness, despair, dread, and fear. The psalmist cries out to God, voicing these emotions, asking for help and relief.

There are about seventy such laments in the book of Psalms and there are more laments than any other kind of genre in the Psalms. Some laments are community laments, written for the nation of Israel as a whole. These psalms address the troubles faced by the community such as when enemy nations threatened them. Other laments were written to voice the troubles of an individual person, such as when David was on the run from Saul. These individual psalms were the private prayers and grief-stricken songs of individual persons, which were then ultimately claimed and sung by the community as a whole.

Though there are many reasons for the psalmist to cry out to God, there tend to be three main complaints or reasons for him to pen his lament. First, he might have been troubled by his own thoughts or actions. 'O Lord, be gracious to me; heal me, for I have sinned against you!' (Ps. 41:4). Secondly, he might have cried out because of the actions of others toward him. 'Vindicate me, O God, and defend my cause against an ungodly people, from the deceitful and unjust man deliver me!' (Ps. 43:1). David wrote psalms such as these while on the run from his enemies. Thirdly, he might have written his lament to voice his frustrations with God Himself. 'Why, O Lord, do you stand far away? Why do you hide yourself in times of trouble?' (Ps. 10:1). These are the laments that cry out to God asking where He is, has He forgotten the psalmist, and will He abandon him forever.[6]

In addition to its dark mood and common complaints, there are other characteristics often

---

6.   Longman. *How to Read the Psalms*, p. 26.

found in the laments. These characteristics are rarely found in all the laments but several or more of these characteristics are found in each lament. We will look at some of these characteristics in more detail later in our journey.

1. *An Invocation*: The invocation is the psalmist's initial cry out to God. 'Hear a just cause, O Lord; attend to my cry! Give ear to my prayer from lips free of deceit!' (Ps. 17:1).

2. *A Plea to God for help*: This is where the psalmist asks for help. If he needs rescue, he asks for rescue. Whatever he needs, he asks for it. 'In your righteousness deliver me and rescue me; incline your ear to me, and save me!' (Ps. 71:2).

3. *Complaints*: This is where the psalmist explains why he is crying out to God to begin with. Perhaps he's been unjustly mistreated. Perhaps he is in deep despair and doesn't know what to do. Perhaps he feels as though God has deserted him. 'Reproaches have broken my heart, so that I am in despair. I looked for pity, but there was none, and for comforters, but I found none. They gave me poison for food, and for my thirst they gave me sour wine to drink' (Ps. 69:20-21).

4. *Curse against his enemies*: This is often seen in psalms where the psalmist is unjustly hunted and pursued by those who desire to harm him. 'May the creditor seize all that he has; may strangers plunder the fruits of his toil! Let there be none to extend kindness to him, nor any to pity his fatherless children!' (Ps. 109:11-12).

5. *Confession of sin or an assertion of innocence*: In some laments, the psalmist will confess wrongdoing. In laments where the psalmist is being unjustly accused or wronged, he will assert his innocence. 'O God, you know my folly; the wrongs I have done are not hidden from you' (Ps. 69:5).

6. *Confidence in what God will do*: The psalmist here turns his attention to God's promises, the character of God, and what God has done in the past. He voices his trust in God, believing that God would indeed be his salvation. 'Behold, God is my helper; the Lord is the upholder of my life' (Ps. 54:4).

7. *Hymn or blessing*: Most psalms end in some form of praise. 'Salvation belongs to the LORD; your blessing be on your people! *Selah*' (Ps. 3:8).[7]

Three-Part Structure of the Laments

All of the laments, except two, follow a structure. They move in a forward trajectory. The laments, though negative in tone, move from the negative to the positive. The psalmist did not write his words simply for the sake of catharsis; there was an ultimate end or goal: trust and worship.

This is our journey as well. We too are going to move from the deep pits of despair to the joy that comes with the morning sun. We are going to learn, study, and follow a three-part structure of the laments so that we can in turn voice our own laments. The structure we will follow is this:

---

7.   Longman. *How to Read the Psalms*, p.26.

1. Crying out to God

2. Asking for help

3. Responding in trust and praise

The next few chapters will unpack this structure in detail.

For Your Heart

1. Read a Psalm of Lament (Ps. 13, 25, 42, or 69), and see if you can find some of the characteristics we looked at above.

2. Are there times in your life that you have failed to lament? Why? What do you think keeps you from lamenting to God?

3. What do you need to lament right now?

6

Crying Out to God

I first met Despair when I was a teen. It began when my grandmother died unexpectedly of a heart attack. Then my best friend one day decided she didn't want to be friends anymore. A serious dating relationship ended with no explanation. I switched schools. My father lost his job, stretching our already thin budget to the point where there was not enough money for food. My parents' already troubled marriage only worsened.

The combination of all these circumstances was like being out on a boat and getting caught in a ferocious storm at sea. I felt as though my life was swirling, spinning, and out of control. The storms of life tore at me until I felt like I would drown.

Many months I spent in that place of darkness. It was a place of loneliness, fear, and sorrow. I found myself crying all the time. I gained a significant amount of weight in a short time. Whenever I was not at work or school, I buried myself in my room where I was enveloped by such deep despair that I desperately wished my life would end.

In college, I learned from a counselor that what I experienced was *depression*. Until that point, I did not have a name for it. But in hearing my experience given a name, I had a sort of 'Aha' moment where everything lined up into place and suddenly made sense.

Despair (depression) and I have met more than once since my adolescence. Following the births of both of my children, that same suffocating darkness enclosed around me. It was like a stalker that never left me out of its sight. I felt trapped with nowhere to go.

Yet there was one common source of comfort during both my adolescent years and those following the births of my sons, the Psalms. I lived in the Psalms as a teenager. It was like David was my counselor; he knew just what I was feeling. Every time I came across a psalm that mirrored my own dark feelings, I wrote it down. Over time, I started penning my own laments.

Then as an adult, I drew strength from the Psalms again. I returned to those well-worn pages of Scripture and revisited words that had meant so much to me as a teen. This time I read the laments with a greater understanding of how God works, the gospel, and a heart that knew from experience that God does indeed hear the cries of a hurting heart.

The Anatomy of our Soul

I think most believers can attest to finding comfort during a trial while reading the Psalms. That's because the words penned by the psalmists reflect the same feelings in our own heart. Though centuries have passed, and though our experiences are far different from those of David and the other writers, we are united by common human emotions. Fear. Loneliness. Sorrow. Anger. Shame. Abandonment. We've all been there and we've all felt these feelings at some point and to some degree.

John Calvin, in his commentary on the Psalms, says this about the way the psalmists speak to our emotions:

> I have been accustomed to call this book, I think not inappropriately, 'An Anatomy of all the Parts of the Soul'; for there is not an emotion of which any one can be conscious that is not here represented as in a mirror. Or rather, the Holy Spirit has here drawn to the life all the griefs, sorrows, fears, doubts, hopes, cares, perplexities, in short, all the distracting emotions with which the minds of men are wont to be agitated.[1]

---

1.   Calvin, John. *Commentary on the Psalms*, http://www.ccel.org/ccel/calvin/calcom08.vi.html, (accessed December 19, 2014).

The Psalms are indeed a mirror, reflecting what is going on inside of us. The Psalms of Lament in particular reflect the darkest of feelings we experience in this fallen world. In this chapter, we are going to look at a few of these laments and narrow in on the first step of our journey: expressing our feelings to God.

Our Savior Felt Things Too

Before we do that, we need to remember that we are not alone in our emotions. When we feel emotions such as sorrow, fear, loneliness or abandonment, we need to remember that our Savior knew such pain Himself.

Jesus was called the 'Man of Sorrows' in Isaiah (53:3). He wept at the tomb of Lazarus (John 11:35). He grieved over the faithlessness of Jerusalem saying, 'O Jerusalem, Jerusalem, the city that kills the prophets and stones those who are sent to it! How often would I have gathered your children together as a hen gathers her brood under her wings, and you were not willing!' (Luke 13:34). He felt the sting of Peter's rejection. 'But Peter said, "Man, I do not know what you are talking about." And immediately, while he was still speaking, the rooster crowed. And the Lord turned and looked at Peter. And Peter remembered the saying of the Lord, how he had said to him, "Before the rooster crows today, you will deny me three times."'(Luke 22:60-61). And He experienced the hellish torture of being separated and abandoned by His Father at the cross.

When we come to God with our feelings, we do not come to a God who is unfamiliar with painful emotions. Hebrews tells us, 'For we do not have a high priest who is unable to sympathize with our weaknesses, but one who in every respect has been tempted as we are, yet without sin' (4:15). Our Lord knew the heavy weight of sorrow and fear, so much so that He sweated drops of blood in the Garden of Gethsemane as He considered what was to come at the cross.

Christ is a savior who knows what it is to feel, yet who in His feelings, never sinned. In His righteousness, He became the perfect sacrifice and substitute for our sins. For all the times that we express our feelings in a sinful way, Jesus' perfect life is credited to us. For all the times we have worried and feared, Jesus' perfect faith and trust in His Father are given to our account. For all the times we are weighed down by sorrow and grief, Jesus stands there as our Savior, who has bought us and redeemed us and calls us His own.

And because of Jesus, we are able to come before the Father in full confidence. Hebrews 4 goes on to say, 'Let us then with confidence draw near to the throne of grace, that we may receive mercy and find grace to help in time of need' (v. 16). Jesus calls us to bring our sorrows to Him. He calls us to cast our cares on Him. Whatever emotions are on your heart, bring them to the throne of grace.

Now let's take a look at a psalm where the writer does just that.

The Not-Yet-King on the Run

Imagine you are the youngest in your family. As the youngest, you are also the least important. In fact, so unimportant that when the local prophet comes to town to worship with your family, you aren't even invited. There you are out in the fields, doing your job of tending to the sheep. It's a job you put your whole heart into. You do whatever it takes to protect your fluffy white charges from danger. You feed your sheep, watch over them, and lead them from one pasture to the next. You even play the harp to keep them calm after a close call with a lion.

Despite your dedication to your work, you are still the youngest. Your brothers on the other hand are tall and strong. They are warriors, fighting for the king of Israel. So when Samuel the prophet comes to anoint the next king, everyone assumes he would want to anoint the oldest and strongest (see 1 Sam. 16). Yet that's not who God has in mind for the job. One by one, Samuel goes down the line of brothers until he gets to last one and finds that none of them is the one God has chosen. He asks the dad, Jesse, 'Have you no more sons?' 'Well,' Jesse responds, 'there is one more. But he's just a shepherd.'

'Bring him here,' Samuel says. As it turns out, that young, unimportant shepherd is the one God has chosen. Samuel anoints the youthful David and then leaves.

David doesn't immediately become king. First he plays the harp for Saul in the palace, soothing the moody and raging king. Then he steps up to fight the mighty Philistine giant, Goliath, and wins. Following that win, Saul hears the women singing about David, comparing him to Saul and becomes jealous and angry. From then on, Saul determines to kill David. So David goes on the run for fear of his life. While hiding in a cave from Saul and his men, he wrote this Psalm of Lament:

> With my voice I cry out to the LORD; with my voice I plead for mercy to the Lord. I pour out my complaint before him; I tell my trouble before him. When my spirit faints within me, you know my way! In the path where I walk they have hidden a trap for me. Look to the right and see: there is none who takes notice of me; no refuge remains to me; no one cares for my soul. I cry to you, O LORD; I say, 'You are my refuge, my portion in the land of the living.' Attend to my cry, for I am brought very low! Deliver me from my persecutors, for they are too strong for me! Bring me out of prison, that I may give thanks to your name! The righteous will surround me, for you will deal bountifully with me (Ps. 142).

Bringing our Feelings to God

One of the greatest lessons we can learn from the Psalms is the importance of expressing our feelings to God. We learn not only of its importance but also the fact that we are free to do so and that God wants us to. Christianity is the only religion that proclaims a God of love who cares about His people. We worship a God who wants us to come to Him with all our cares. This is an extraordinary and marvelous truth. Soak that in for a moment: the God of the universe, the all-eternal, always existent One, who spoke the world into existence, who makes the clouds a footstool for His feet, desires that we come into His presence.

In earlier chapters, we looked at the origins of our difficult and painful feelings. Because of the fall, life is painful and hard. We will experience suffering and trials. We will grieve, have sorrow, and feel fear. We also looked in greater detail at the various ways we tend to handle our feelings. We cover them up, hide them, stuff them, and try to make them go away. We may bury ourselves in our work. We might feed our feelings by digging into a pint of ice cream. We might try and take control of our problems in the hope that it will relieve our pain. Sometimes, we use our feelings to attack others. We may lash out at loved ones. We might even lay blame on others for our problems.

Yet the Psalms of Lament show us another way. They show us that we need to bring our feelings to God. When we are suffering, when we've been hurt by someone else, when we've lost all that we hold dear, when our dreams have been dashed, when the trials of life are overwhelming, we need to bring it all to God. Whatever they are, the good, bad, and the ugly, we need to bring our feelings to Him.

John Calvin, in his commentary on Psalm 142 wrote:

> To pour out one's thoughts and tell over his afflictions implies the reverse of those perplexing anxieties which men brood over inwardly to their own distress, and by which they torture themselves, and are chafed by their afflictions rather than led to God; or it implies the reverse of those frantic exclamations to which others give utterance who find no comfort in the superintending providence and care of God. In short, we are left to infer that while he did not give way before men to loud and

senseless lamentations, neither did he suffer himself
to be tormented with inward and suppressed cares,
but made known his griefs with unsuspecting
confidence to the Lord.[2]

David was in fear for his life but he didn't stuff
his feelings, tormenting himself with 'inward and
suppressed cares,' nor did he cry out in hysterics to
his fellow men in 'loud and senseless lamentations.'
Instead, he took his griefs to God in prayer.

Being Honest with God

The next important element that the laments teach
us is *how* to bring our feelings to God. The laments
are raw, unfiltered, and real. They do not pretend
that everything is OK when it clearly is not. The
writers of these laments come to God just as they are
and tell Him exactly what is going on in their hearts.

After all, God already knows what is going on in
us. There is no need to hide or pretend with Him. He
is omniscient, knowing everything we are thinking
and feeling even before we do. As David wrote
elsewhere in the Psalms, 'Even before a word is on
my tongue, behold, O Lord, you know it altogether'
(139:4). In Jeremiah, God proclaimed, 'Can a man
hide himself in secret places so that I cannot see him?
declares the Lord. Do I not fill heaven and earth?
declares the Lord' (23:24).

In Psalm 142, we see that David's lament is
honest. He is transparent, revealing the depths of

---

2.   Calvin, John. *Commentary on the Psalms*, http://biblehub.
     com/library/calvin/commentary_on_psalms_volume_5/
     psalm_142_1-4.htm, (accessed December 20, 2014).

his pain. He was real and truthful about how he felt and to what extent he felt it. He writes in verse 1, 'I cry aloud ... I pour out my complaint ... I tell my trouble.' In verse 4, he laments that no one seems to care about him, 'No one is concerned for me ... no one cares for my life.' In verse 6 David writes, 'I am in desperate need.'

In our day and age, we tend to not fully experience or acknowledge our feelings for what they are. To admit to ourselves or to others that we have any kind of weakness is just not acceptable. But any time we deny the reality of something, it only delays the inevitable. Sooner or later, the truth comes out.

We once did a fun science experiment with our kids where we made Alka-Seltzer grenades. In a plastic soda bottle, we combined Alka-Seltzer and vinegar. Quickly screwing on the lid, we then threw the bottles onto the ground and watched them explode. The combination of Alka-Seltzer and vinegar reacts to form a gas which then builds up pressure. Since there's not enough room in the plastic bottle to contain the gas, it explodes.

This is what often happens to our emotions when we try to deny their existence. Pressure builds up and our feelings explode. For some of us, the explosion hurts others around us, and for others, we only end up hurting ourselves.

The laments encourage us to instead face our feelings, look at them, give them names, acknowledge them and be honest about them. The laments give us permission and freedom to feel. They acknowledge that we are humans and that we have feelings. While it's true that our feelings are not always an accurate indicator of reality and often they exaggerate things (which we will discuss in a later chapter), our feelings do tell us something. They tell us that something is wrong. As we move forward in our journey, we'll see that the laments are about more than simple catharsis. Lamenting to God isn't only about venting our feelings. But it is the first step and an important one.

When we find ourselves faced with difficult feelings, we need to acknowledge them. We need to name them. We need to be descriptive, using as many adjectives as we can think of. Here are a few more examples of naming specific feelings in the laments:

> You have put me in the depths of the pit, in the regions dark and deep. Your wrath lies heavy upon me, and you overwhelm me with all your waves. You have caused my companions to shun me; you have made me a horror to them. I am shut in so that I cannot escape; my eye grows dim through sorrow (Ps. 88:6-9a).

Here David voices feelings of hopelessness. He feels trapped, alone, and overwhelmed.

> How long, O LORD? Will you forget me forever? How long will you hide your face from me? How long must I take counsel in my soul and have sorrow in my heart all the day? How long shall my enemy be exalted over me? (Ps. 13:1-2).

In this psalm, David expresses feelings of abandonment and sorrow.

In Psalm 22, David voices feelings of worthlessness. He feels despised and hated:

> But I am a worm and not a man, scorned by
> mankind and despised by the people. All who see
> me mock me; they make mouths at me; they wag
> their heads (vv. 6-7).

Ask the Hard Questions

Another aspect to the laments is the hard questions the writer asks. Not only should we be honest and descriptive about the way we feel, but we also need to ask God all the hard questions on our hearts.

In Psalm 13, David asks the question, 'How long, O Lord?' This is a question many of us ask. How long until we meet the man we are to marry? How long will we have to wait until we can finally pay off that debt? How long will we be sick? How long until our prodigal child returns home? How long until we no longer feel lonely, depressed, or afraid?

'How long?' is the cry of God's people through the centuries. It began the day Adam and Eve were barred from Eden, clinging to the hope and promise that one day a Savior would come and crush the head of the serpent. It was a cry echoed by the Hebrews during their tenure of slavery in Egypt. Though the cry was answered with the Son of God's own cry from the cross, 'It is finished!' it is still the cry of believers who are waiting for the final consummation of Christ's redemption and restoration. The question, 'How long?' even rings out in the halls of heaven as the souls of the martyred cry out, 'O Sovereign Lord, holy and true, how long before you will judge and avenge our blood on those who dwell on the earth?' (Rev. 6:10).

Another question that is often on our hearts is 'Why?' When the pains of life come and cut into our lives, we want to know why. The psalmist asked the same question, 'O God, why do you cast us off forever? Why does your anger smoke against the sheep of your pasture?' (74:1). 'Why?' is the question Job asked following the loss of nearly everything in his life. It is also the question our Savior cried out from the cross, quoting a psalm of David, 'My God, my God, why have you forsaken me?' (Ps. 22:1a).

Whatever hard questions are stirring your heart, bring them to God. He already knows them. Be honest about your pain. Follow the pattern of the laments and cry out before Him. Ask God, 'Why?' 'How long?' 'When?' 'Who?' 'What?' and every other question on your heart.

When there are No Words

Sometimes, in the midst of our deep pain, there are no words. Sometimes, the pain is so deep, the horror so real, we can barely breathe, much less put our feelings into words. This is when we trust in the great grace of Christ. Paul tells us in the book of Romans that when we can't give voice or words to our pain, the Holy Spirit is interceding for us. 'Likewise the Spirit helps us in our weakness. For we do not know what to pray for as we ought, but the Spirit himself intercedes for us with groanings too deep for words' (8:26).

What marvelous grace and love! Even when we are weak and cannot express the deepest cries of our heart, the Spirit is going before the Father on our behalf, speaking for us. And the words He speaks are perfect, holy, and true. We can take great comfort knowing that even when the pains of life mute us, the Spirit is our advocate.

While this is only the first part of our journey, it is still a crucial one. If you have spent your life covering your feelings, hiding them, stuffing them, distracting yourself from them, or taking them out on others, the laments show you there is another way.

Or if expressing your feelings is hard for you, if you've never been able to verbalize or identify what you are feeling, you might want to linger here in this step for a while. Remember, this is a journey; a marathon and not a sprint.

Take the time to feel. Look at all the ways the psalmist describes his feelings. See how honest he is in the questions he asks. Talk with God. Be real. Be raw. And come before the throne of grace in great confidence.

For Your Heart

1. Name some emotions you are feeling right now. What are some painful emotions you have felt in the past? How can you relate with David's emotions?

2. Do you find it hard to express your emotions to God? In what ways do you hide, deny, stuff, or distract yourself from your feelings?

3. What does it mean to you that Christ felt painful emotions as well, that He knows what

it feels like to suffer grief, sorrow, rejection, abandonment?

4. Read Psalm 88 and 102 and write down the different emotions the psalmist expresses.

5. Come before the throne of grace and put your feelings into words in a prayer. Name them and describe them to your heavenly Father who hears you and already knows all that you are thinking and feeling.

7

Asking for Help

When my children were babies, they cried whenever they needed something. They cried when they were hungry. They cried when they were tired. They cried when their belly hurt. They cried to communicate their every need, large or small. I couldn't wait until they were old enough to talk so that I could finally know just what it was they needed. Of course, now their spoken requests never end!

In the last chapter, we looked at being honest before God. This next step in our journey with the psalmist involves asking God for help. It seems like a simple, easy step, but for some of us, asking for help does not come naturally. We are used to relying on ourselves. In a culture where everything we want or need can be provided at the swipe of a credit card or the press of the enter key, it is hard to think of ourselves as dependent creatures. But dependent we are and one of the underlying assumptions in the laments is this aspect of dependency.

Our Utter Dependency

Everything we have comes to us by God's grace. Everything. That includes the air we breathe and our very life itself (Acts 17:25). God holds the world in His hands. All things are governed by His sovereign control. 'He covers the heavens with clouds; he prepares rain for the earth; he makes grass grow on the hills. He gives to the beasts their food, and to the young ravens that cry' (Ps. 147:8-9). 'For behold, he who forms the mountains and creates the wind, and declares to man what is his thought, who makes the morning darkness, and treads on the heights of the earth—the LORD, the God of hosts, is his name!' (Amos 4:13).

We are just as dependent upon God as babies are on their parents. We are dependent upon God for food to eat, jobs to work, children to hold, and a bed to lie on at the end of day. We are also dependent upon His strength, His wisdom, His provision, His direction, His healing, His protection, and His salvation. He gives us all these things out of His abundant grace. We cannot provide any of it for ourselves. Left to our own devices, we would be helpless and useless.

In fact, on our own, we are completely dead in our trespasses and sins. We cannot love God or the things of God. We have to be brought back from the dead and given a new heart. 'And I will give you a new heart, and a new spirit I will put within you. And I will remove the heart of stone from your flesh and give you a heart of flesh. And I will put my Spirit within you, and cause you to walk in my statutes and be careful to obey my rules' (Ezek. 36:26-27). That's the vision Ezekiel saw in the Valley of Dry Bones and the covenant promise given in Jeremiah. This promise was then fulfilled in Christ:

> But God, being rich in mercy, because of the great love with which he loved us, even when we were dead in our trespasses, made us alive together with Christ – by grace you have been saved – and raised us up with him and seated us with him in the heavenly places in Christ Jesus, so that in the coming ages he might show the immeasurable riches of his grace in kindness toward us in Christ Jesus. For by grace you have been saved through faith. And this is not your own doing; it is the gift of God, not a result of works, so that no one may boast. (Eph. 2:4-9)

It is not only our salvation that comes to us by grace, but our sanctification and our perseverance in faith as well. God's work to change and transform us is a work of His grace. It's God's grace from beginning to end. Jesus said in John 15 that we can do nothing apart from

Him. 'Abide in me, and I in you. As the branch cannot
bear fruit by itself, unless it abides in the vine, neither
can you, unless you abide in me. I am the vine; you are
the branches. Whoever abides in me and I in him, he it
is that bears much fruit, for apart from me you can do
nothing' (vv. 4-5). Just as a branch cannot thrive apart
from the vine, neither can we grow, thrive, or produce
fruit apart from Christ. As we remain in Christ, the
Spirit bears fruit in us. He changes us and grows us
in holiness. Like the healthy branch connected to the
tree bears fruit, as we remain connected to the vine of
Christ, we produce fruits of love, joy, peace, patience,
kindness, goodness, faithfulness, gentleness, and self-
control (Gal. 5:22-23).

From our life and breath to our daily provisions;
from our salvation to our sanctification; all things
come to us by God's grace. Understanding this
dependency and our need for God's grace helps us
understand the heart of the laments. The laments
strip us of any and all pretense that we can be our
own savior and that we can do life on our own. They
reveal the truth of our helplessness and our utter need
for mercy and grace. When we lament, it means that
we acknowledge our great need for grace and that we
are turning to the only One who can supply it.

Permission to Ask

This second stage in our journey through the laments
gives us permission to ask God for help. Just as we
need to be open and honest about our emotions when
we come to God, we also need to be honest about what
we need. In the laments, the psalmist does not hesitate
to ask for what he wants. He is specific and direct.

He asks for deliverance:

Turn, O LORD, deliver my life; save me for the sake of your steadfast love. (Ps. 6:4)

Deliver me from sinking in the mire; let me be delivered from my enemies and from the deep waters. Let not the flood sweep over me, or the deep swallow me up, or the pit close its mouth over me. Answer me, O LORD, for your steadfast love is good; according to your abundant mercy, turn to me. Hide not your face from your servant; for I am in distress; make haste to answer me. Draw near to my soul, redeem me; ransom me because of my enemies! (Ps. 69:14-18)

He asks for God's attention:

Consider and answer me, O Lord my God; (Ps. 13:3a)

O God, hear my prayer; give ear to the words of my mouth. (Ps. 54:2)

He asks for justice:

Vindicate me, O God, and defend my cause against an ungodly people, from the deceitful and unjust man deliver me! (Ps. 43:1)

Pour out your indignation upon them, and let your burning anger overtake them. (Ps. 69:24)

He asks for forgiveness:

Wash me thoroughly from my iniquity, and cleanse me from my sin! (Ps. 51:2)

Deliver me from all my transgressions. (Ps. 39:8)

He asks to be in communion with God:

> One thing have I asked of the Lᴏʀᴅ, that will I seek
> after: that I may dwell in the house of the Lord all
> the days of my life, to gaze upon the beauty of the
> Lord and to inquire in his temple. (Ps. 27:4)

> My soul thirsts for God, for the living God. When
> shall I come and appear before God? (Ps. 42:2)

Throughout the laments, the psalmist pours out
his complaints and needs before God. As the *Gospel
Transformation Bible* notes:

> No other faith has a holy book whose writers talk to
> God as the psalmists do. Particularly when it comes
> to suffering, the psalmists make bold complaints
> … [the psalmist] is emboldened to do so because
> he knows God's essential nature is to be merciful
> … David thus provides the follower of Christ an
> inspired vocabulary to express his or her frustration
> with God's painful providence. David also leaves
> a legacy of faith by demonstrating that, when we
> flee to God alone for mercy, our conscience finds
> lasting relief from the trouble of our sins. We lean
> ultimately on God's 'steadfast love' (Ps. 6:4) — love
> that is fulfilled in Jesus Christ.[1]

Why We Can Ask God for Help

This is not the part of the chapter where I preach
the prosperity gospel and tell you that God wants to
give you everything you've ever wanted, you need
only ask. I am not going to tell you that God wants

---

1.   *Gospel Transformation Bible* (Chicago, IL: Crossway, 2013), pp. 658-9.

you to live your best life now, nor that He will take away all your problems and make your life one of comfort and ease. To do so would be inconsistent with Scripture. God is not a candy machine where we dispense our prayers and out comes all that we ask and desire.

But I will tell you that the laments show us that we can cry out to God for rescue and help. Just as my children do not hesitate to tell me when they are hungry or hurt, we can do the same with our Father in heaven. We can ask for a job, for healing, for relationships to be restored, for wisdom, for endurance, for protection, and for anything we need. And we can ask for all of that because of who we are in Christ.

Through faith in Christ's completed work on our behalf, we have been adopted into the family of God. We are heirs of the covenant, grafted into the family tree. 'And if you are Christ's, then you are Abraham's offspring, heirs according to promise' (Gal. 3:29). 'Blessed be the God and Father of our Lord Jesus Christ! According to his great mercy, he has caused us to be born again to a living hope through the resurrection of Jesus Christ from the dead, to an inheritance that is imperishable, undefiled, and unfading, kept in heaven for you' (1 Pet. 1:3-4). God hears us because we are His; we belong to Him. 'But you are a chosen race, a royal priesthood, a holy nation, a people for his own possession, that you may proclaim the excellencies of him who called you out of darkness into his marvelous light. Once you were not a people, but now you are God's people;

once you had not received mercy, but now you have received mercy' (1 Pet. 2:9-10).

He is a God who cares for His children. He knows all the hair on our head and keeps our tears in a bottle. We are more important than the birds of the air and the flowers in the fields, all of whom He provides for in abundance. 'Look at the birds of the air; they neither sow nor reap nor gather into barns, and yet your heavenly Father feeds them. Are you not of more value than they?' (Matt. 6:26). Just as we seek to provide all that our own children need, our heavenly Father seeks our good as well; only His provisions for us are perfect, righteous, and holy. 'If you then, who are evil, know how to give good gifts to your children, how much more will your Father who is in heaven give good things to those who ask him!' (Matt. 7:11).

Relish the truth that you are a child of God. The gospel has changed you from a homeless orphan to a child with a forever family. Christ will never leave you nor forsake you. Because of that glorious truth, take time to consider what it is that you need. What are your physical, emotional, and spiritual needs? If you are in a relationship that is suffering, ask God for restoration. If you are sick, pray for healing. If you need work, pray for that. If your heart is breaking, ask for peace and joy. If you feel far from God, ask Him to draw you near to Him. Whatever you need, ask.

The Right Motives

As we consider our needs, it is a good time to also consider our motives. James says, 'You desire and do not have, so you murder. You covet and cannot obtain, so you fight and quarrel. You do not have, because you do not ask. You ask and do not receive, because you ask wrongly, to spend it on your passions' (4:2-3). James is telling us two things here. We don't have because we don't ask. We just covered the glorious reasons on why we can ask. Now let's look at what else James tells us, 'because you ask wrongly.'

Because we are sinful, even the good things we ask for can be marred by sin. So many of the good things God has created for our enjoyment can become first things in our heart, above God Himself. That job we hope and pray for – while work is a necessary and good thing for us to have – can easily become our first thing. We can think in our heart, 'I'll be happy once I have that job.' Or that marriage we want – also a good thing – can become an idol in our heart where we think that it alone can make us happy, fulfilled, and complete.

The *Westminster Confession* tells us that the chief end of man is to 'glorify God and enjoy him forever.' We were made to love and worship our Creator. God enjoyed the perfect love and fellowship within the Triune Godhead so much that He wanted to share it with us. He wanted us to enter into that same love and fellowship God the Father, God the Son, and God the Holy Spirit has enjoyed from all eternity. But because of sin, we don't live out what we were created to do. We don't love God with all our heart, soul, mind, and strength. We don't worship and glorify Him as He deserves.

Our hearts have turned from our one true love. We have wandered far from Him, seeking ways to fill the void that only God can fill. As Augustine said, 'Thou hast made us for thyself, and our heart is restless until it finds its rest in thee.' When God alone isn't the source of our satisfaction and the longing of our heart, we seek to fill our longings somewhere else. Our restless hearts fill the 'God-shaped hole' in our heart with love for things, experiences, people, pleasures, and responses from others. As John Calvin said, our hearts are idol-making factories. We can turn anything into an idol and bow down before it. Though our idols are not made of wood or stone, they are idols just the same, robbing the affections that belong to God alone. Such idols consume our thoughts and our energies. They are things that become so central to our life that if we didn't have them, we would be devastated.

Perhaps you are unsure if what you are asking God for is an idol or not. Sometimes idols can be hard to identify. They can grow like weeds in our heart, like an invasive vine that wraps and twists itself around trees until all you can see is the vine and not the trees. Tim Keller provides multiple suggestions for determining whether there is an idol in our heart in his book, *Counterfeit Gods*. One test is this:

> Look at your most uncontrollable emotions. Just as the fisherman looking for fish knows to go where the water is roiling, look for your idols at the bottom of your most painful emotions, especially those that never seem to lift and that drive you to do things that you know are wrong. If you are angry, ask, 'Is there something here too important to me, something I must have at all costs?' Do the same

thing with strong fear or despair and guilt. Ask yourself, 'Am I so scared, because something in my life is being threatened that I think is a necessity when it is not? Am I so down on myself because I have lost or failed at something that I think is a necessity when it is not?' ... When you ask questions like that, when you 'pull your emotions up by the roots,' as it were, you will often find your idols clinging to them.[2]

Journeying through the laments helps us to pause and evaluate the motives of our heart. Why do we ask? What do we hope to get? Is our hope centered on God or on what He can give us? And what if He says no? Can we say with the prophet, 'Though the fig tree should not blossom, nor fruit be on the vines, the produce of the olive fail and the fields yield no food, the flock be cut off from the fold and there be no herd in the stalls, yet I will rejoice in the LORD; I will take joy in the God of my salvation' (Hab. 3:17-18). Or with the psalmist, 'God is our refuge and strength, a very present help in trouble. Therefore we will not fear though the earth gives way, though the mountains be moved into the heart of the sea, though its waters roar and foam, though the mountains tremble at its swelling' (46:1-3).

If we find that the motives of our heart stem from an idol or counterfeit love of our heart, we need to repent. We need to acknowledge our sin and seek God's forgiveness. Repentance requires turning away

---

2. Keller, Timothy. *Counterfeit Gods: The Empty Promises of Money, Sex, and Power, and the Only Hope That Matters* (New York, NY: Dutton, 2009), pp. 169-70.

from our sin. In turning from our idols, we have to
turn toward something else. And that something else
is Christ. As Tim Keller wrote, 'Jesus must become
more beautiful to your imagination, more attractive
to your heart, than your idol. That is what will replace
your counterfeit gods. If you uproot the idol and fail
to "plant" the love of Christ in its place, the idol will
grow back.'[3]

Pray that God would help you identify the idols
in your heart. Pray that Christ alone would be the
greatest desire of your heart. Focus your heart on
Christ and His great love for you in the gospel. Then
the promise spoken of by the psalmist will be true
for you, 'Delight yourself in the LORD, and he will
give you the desires of your heart' (37:4).

Keep Asking

Now that we have looked at motives and idols of
the heart, let's talk about another aspect we see in
how the psalmist asks for help. He didn't only ask
God one time for help and then stop. We see in the
laments that he sought God over and over. 'O LORD,
God of my salvation; I cry out day and night before
you. Let my prayer come before you; incline your
ear to my cry!' (Ps. 88:1-2). 'How long, O LORD? Will
you forget me forever? How long will you hide your
face from me?' (Ps. 13:1).

In the book of Luke, Jesus encouraged such persist-
ent prayer, 'And he told them a parable to the effect
that they ought always to pray and not lose heart. He

---

3.   Keller. *Counterfeit Gods: The Empty Promises of Money, Sex, and
      Power, and the Only Hope That Matters*, p. 172.

said, "In a certain city there was a judge who neither feared God nor respected man. And there was a widow in that city who kept coming to him and saying, 'Give me justice against my adversary.' For a while he refused, but afterward he said to himself, 'Though I neither fear God nor respect man, yet because this widow keeps bothering me, I will give her justice, so that she will not beat me down by her continual coming.'" And the Lord said, "Hear what the unrighteous judge says. And will not God give justice to his elect, who cry to him day and night? Will he delay long over them? I tell you, he will give justice to them speedily. Nevertheless, when the Son of Man comes, will he find faith on earth?" ' (18:1-8).

We know that Paul prayed three times for his 'thorn in the flesh' to be removed. Our Savior, on the night before He died, persisted in His own prayer of lament. In the Garden of Gethsemane, He asked the Father to take the cup of wrath away from Him. Multiple times He prayed, 'Abba, Father, all things are possible for you. Remove this cup from me. Yet not what I will, but what you will' (Mark 14:36). He yielded to God's will for our sakes so that we would be redeemed.

Unlike Paul, we probably won't get such a clear response as he did. And unlike Christ, we don't know the complete and full plan God has for us. So keep praying and keep asking. And wait for His response.

While You Wait

The laments are a journey and often that journey involves waiting. Sometimes in God's great wisdom and plan, He desires for us to stay in that place of need where we have to continually cry out to Him. He might not respond right away to our pleas for help. Like Job, sometimes we have to live in a season of lament and grief while we wait for the Lord to respond.

If you have cried out to God and voiced your deepest hurts and sorrows and then asked for His help, you are now in a season of waiting. It is in this season where the real work is done and what will lead you to the final step in the three-part structure of the laments which we will look at in the next chapter.

As you wait:

1. *Don't give up*: When we are in a season of waiting, it is tempting to doubt God's goodness and faithfulness and attempt to take things under our control. This is what the Israelites did in Exodus 32 when Moses was on the mountain receiving the law of God. They waited at the base of the mountain, wondering when Moses would return. 'When the people saw that Moses delayed to come down from the mountain, the people gathered themselves together to Aaron and said to him, "Up, make us gods who shall go before us. As for this Moses, the man who brought us up out of the land of Egypt, we do not know what has become of him"' (32:1). So Aaron gathered gold from all the people and created a golden calf for them to worship.

The Israelites gave up on waiting and took things into their own hands. They used their time of waiting to sin against God by creating a golden calf. During seasons of waiting on God to answer, don't give up and turn your heart away from Him. Don't seek to find your answer apart from Him.

2. *Instead, glorify God while you wait*: Seasons of waiting are not times where we sit around and wait for God to write an answer in the sky, showing us which way to go. We are to actively live out our faith, even while we wait. God can use us even as we stand at a crossroads in our life. Scripture tells us to glorify God in all that we do, that includes seasons of waiting.

The late missionary, Jim Elliot, is known as saying, 'Wherever you are, be all there.' We don't know how long our season of waiting is. Maybe it will end tomorrow; maybe it will go on for an extended period of time. We need to be fully present in today. We need to glorify God, pursue the works of the Kingdom, live faithfully for Christ, wherever we are and for however long we are there.

3. *Read God's Word*: God communicates with us through His written Word. As we read and study, the Spirit will use God's Word to speak to our hearts, showing us His will. While you wait for His answer, stay in the Word. Seek to grow in your knowledge of God. Seek to understand the way He works in our lives. Seek to know more of God's love for you through Christ. All of that is done through reading God's inspired Word.

As you read, pray this prayer of Paul's: 'that the God of our Lord Jesus Christ, the Father of glory, may give you the Spirit of wisdom and of revelation in the knowledge of him, having the eyes of your hearts enlightened, that you may know what is the hope to which he has called you, what are the riches of his glorious inheritance in the saints, and what is the immeasurable greatness of his power toward us who believe, according to the working of his great might that he worked in Christ when he raised him from the dead and seated him at his right hand in the heavenly places, far above all rule and authority and power and dominion, and above every name that is named, not only in this age but also in the one to come' (Eph. 1:17-21).

4. *Remember that God is not out to get you*: Sometimes we can think that God is making us wait for an answer because He is out to get us. We think that it is some form of punishment and that He is angry with us. Romans 8:1 says, 'there is therefore now no condemnation for those who are in Christ Jesus.' God already emptied His wrath on Christ at the cross. He is not out to get us. He may use a season of waiting for discipline or training, but it is not out of anger and wrath.

5. *Waiting is good for us*: Lamentations 3:26 says that it is good to wait for the salvation of the Lord. Romans 8:28 promises that God uses all things – including waiting – for our spiritual good. We are being conformed into the image of Christ and it is during seasons of waiting where great things can happen. Even when He seems silent, God is always at work in us through His Spirit. And in that place of waiting, He often uses that time to show us our sin and to strip us of that sin. God uses that time of waiting to draw us deeper into His grace. As we stand there at the crossroads of life, waiting for His answer, we learn to cling to Him, to trust, and to

hope. For as the psalmist encourages us, 'Be strong, and let your heart take courage, all you who wait for the LORD' (31:24).

6. *Do what comes next*: Sometimes we can become immobilized and frozen while we wait for God. We don't know what to do, so we do nothing. The truth is, we can't just sit in the waiting room of life and watch life pass us by. We have to keep moving forward. Sometimes, when we don't know what else to do, we need to do what comes next. We need to feed our children, go to work, run errands, do laundry, pay the bills, and do all the daily tasks of life.

God has not forgotten you. His intentions toward you are good. He knows exactly what you need right now in this moment. You need more of Him. You need Christ. You need gospel hope, gospel confidence, and gospel joy. And that is what we will find in the next step of our journey.

For Your Heart

1. Read Psalms 5–7. Write down everything the psalmist asks for. What kinds of things does he ask for? Are there common themes? Do you see his heart of dependence upon God's mercy?

2. What do you need to ask God for help with right now?

3. Do you struggle with depending on God for all things? Why or why not?

4. Pray through and consider the idols in your heart. Ask for God to help you pull them out and replace them with greater love and affection for Christ.

5. What can you do right now while you wait for God to answer your cries for help?

8

Responding in Trust and Worship

We are now at the last part of the three-part structure we are following in the laments. This is the part of the journey where our emotions are reshaped. We entered the journey overwhelmed and overcome by our emotions. We learned to voice those emotions to our Heavenly Father. We cried out to Him and asked for Him to rescue us, save us, and heal us.

In this final step, we move from fear to trust; from despair to joy; from shame to confidence.

A Sharp Turn

There's a road in the mountains of Tennessee that our family likes to ride on when we travel in the southern United States. I should say that my husband likes to drive on the road, the rest of us just hold on tight. The road is aptly named the 'W Road' because it is in the shape of 'W.' When you get to the points in the 'W' you have to go extra slow to make sure you can make it through the tight turns and not hit someone coming down the mountain from the other direction. The turns are sharp and steep and if you've never been on the road before, it can be terrifying to drive.

Perhaps you have traveled on an unfamiliar road before. Some roads can veer sharp when you least expect it. Everyone holds on tight as you steer hard to stay on the road. That's kind of what happens in this last stage of the laments. As we read through the laments, sometimes it seems as though the psalmist has all of a sudden made a wild, hairpin turn. His change in direction seems to come out of nowhere.

We followed along as he poured out his emotions. We nodded our head at his requests for help. We understood all of that. Then we get to the end of the lament and we find the psalmist is praising God. He ends his lament with a worshipful tone that just seems out of place. We wonder, just how did he get there?

The important thing to note at the outset of this chapter is that while the psalmist's abrupt change seems out of place, the truth is, we don't see the entire internal journey he took to get there. It takes us mere moments to read the psalm, so it seems to us to be tight and neat and wrapped up nicely, not unlike a television show where the crisis or mystery is solved at the end of every episode. Yet the reality is, the circumstances in the life of the psalmist took place over a period of time. He went through a journey that took longer than it does for us to read it. As Tremper Longman wrote, 'It sometimes appears that the psalmist changed his negative feelings to positive ones in a brief moment, but this isn't how it happened. The Psalms compress time in such a way that what was a long process appears as a sudden insight. Honest emotional struggle stands behind the Psalms.'[1]

Let's look at a lament to see this sharp turn and what we can learn from it.

Psalm 13

Psalm 13 is a short psalm that shows us this abrupt move:

> How long, O Lord? Will you forget me forever?
>> How long will you hide your face from me?
> How long must I take counsel in my soul
>> and have sorrow in my heart all the day?
> How long shall my enemy be exalted over me?
>
> Consider and answer me, O Lord my God;
>> light up my eyes, lest I sleep the sleep of death,
> lest my enemy say, "I have prevailed over him,"
>> lest my foes rejoice because I am shaken.

---

1. Longman. *How to Read the Psalms*, p. 81.

> But I have trusted in your steadfast love;
> 　　my heart shall rejoice in your salvation.
> I will sing to the LORD,
> 　　because he has dealt bountifully with me.

The beginning of this psalm has the psalmist pouring out his heart. He feels abandoned. 'Will you forget me forever?' he asks. He is filled with sorrow. He asks the question all our hearts ask, 'How long?' Then he asks God to move in his life to answer him and to revive him. 'Look on me and answer, LORD my God.'

It is in the last section of this psalm where the psalmist makes that sharp turn. 'But I trust in your unfailing love; my heart rejoices in your salvation.' The psalmist ends with a response of trust in God. He worships and praises God, 'I will sing the LORD's praise, for he has been good to me.'

What happened that brought about that change? What took place in the psalmist's heart that brought about that restoration of trust and compelled him to respond in worship? In this particular psalm and in others, there are a couple of clues that reveal to us what might have taken place.

God's Unfailing Love

One of the things the psalmist looks to in Psalm 13 is God's great love for him. 'But I trust in your unfailing love.' He turns to what he knows to be true about God. In the shadowy darkness when all he hears is the echo of his own beating heart, the psalmist feels all alone. He has cried out to God but God has been silent. He doesn't know when or why or how God will respond and intervene. In that quietness, he turns to what he knows about God: God is love.

As an Israelite steeped in the stories of God's covenant love, the psalmist knew of God's great love for His people. He knew what happened to Moses when he hid behind the rock and saw God's back as He walked by. 'The LORD passed before him and proclaimed, "The LORD, the LORD, a God merciful and gracious, slow to anger, and abounding in steadfast love and faithfulness",' (Exod. 34:6). He knew that God had set His love on the Israelites and chosen them to be His people. 'It was not because you were more in number than any other people that the LORD set his love on you and chose you, for you were the fewest of all peoples, but it is because the LORD loves you' (Deut. 7:7-8a).

The love of God is a recurring frame throughout both the Old and New Testaments.

> The LORD is merciful and gracious, slow to anger and abounding in steadfast love. (Ps. 103:8)

> And he prayed to the LORD and said, 'O LORD, is not this what I said when I was yet in my country? That is why I made haste to flee to Tarshish; for I knew that you are a gracious God and merciful, slow to anger and abounding in steadfast love, and relenting from disaster.'(Jonah 4:2)

> Beloved, let us love one another, for love is from God, and whoever loves has been born of God and knows God. Anyone who does not love does not know God, because God is love. In this the love of God was made manifest among us, that God sent his only Son into the world, so that we might live through him. In this is love, not that we have loved

> God but that he loved us and sent his Son to be the
> propitiation for our sins. (1 John 4:7-10)

> Blessed be the God and Father of our Lord Jesus
> Christ, who has blessed us in Christ with every
> spiritual blessing in the heavenly places, even as he
> chose us in him before the foundation of the world,
> that we should be holy and blameless before him.
> In love he predestined us for adoption as sons
> through Jesus Christ, according to the purpose of
> his will. (Eph. 1:3-5)

God's love for us is immeasurable and limitless. It is
not dependent on anything we have done. There is
nothing we can do to make Him love us more or love
us any less. His love originates within the Triune
Godhead and it's a love He has chosen to share with
us. And unlike the love we have for others, God's
love is unconditional, perfect, holy, righteous and
good. It is this love that the psalmist looked to as he
waited for God's response to his lament. Focusing on
God's love helped reshape his emotions. It restored
his trust. And in response to the love of God, he was
able to offer praise and worship.

On this side of the cross, we have seen the apex and
fulfillment of God's love poured out for His people at
the cross. As Paul says in Romans, 'He who did not
spare his own Son but gave him up for us all, how will
he not also with him graciously give us all things?'
(8:32). When we find ourselves in the same place as the
psalmist, we too can focus on God's love for us in Christ.
The more we dwell on God's great love, the more our
own hearts are transformed and we also can respond in
trust and worship. As Mark Futato writes:

You can trust God because he is characterized by unfailing love for you, by a love that will not let you go, by a love that can only do what is the very best for you ... the proof that God has this love for you is seen in his gift of Christ to you. God gave you his Son to live a perfect life in your place, to die on the cross to pay for your sins, and to be raised form the dead to empower you for new life, so it is utterly unthinkable that God would now fail to give you everything else you need.[2]

God as Savior

At the end of Psalm 13, the psalmist wrote, 'my heart rejoices in your salvation.' In addition to dwelling on God's love, the psalmist also put his hope in God as his savior. Many of the Psalms speak of God as a savior, refuge, fortress, and deliverer.

> Deliver me from bloodguiltiness, O God, O God of my salvation, and my tongue will sing aloud of your righteousness. (Ps. 51:14)

> Lead me in your truth and teach me, for you are the God of my salvation; for you I wait all the day long. (Ps. 25:5)

> Trust in him at all times, O people; pour out your heart before him; God is a refuge for us. (Ps. 62:8)

> God is our refuge and strength, a very present help in trouble. (Ps. 46:1)

> The LORD is my rock and my fortress and my deliverer, my God, my rock, in whom I take refuge, my shield, and the horn of my salvation, my stronghold. (Ps. 18:2)

---

2.   Futato. *Joy Comes in the Morning: Psalms for All Seasons*, p. 71.

> Help me, O LORD my God! Save me according to
> your steadfast love! (Ps. 109:26)

> O Israel, hope in the LORD! For with the LORD
> there is steadfast love, and with him is plentiful
> redemption. And he will redeem Israel from all his
> iniquities. (Ps. 130:7-8)

We will look at this in greater detail in a later chapter,
but it is important to note that the psalmist is
reflecting back on God's past faithfulness. He knows
God has delivered and saved His people in the past
and he trusts and believes that God will do so now.
He is putting his trust in the unfailing character of
God as Savior. As we looked at in an earlier chapter,
the laments are written out of an understanding that
we are dependent upon God for His grace toward
us. The psalmist is resting in that dependence,
relying on God to move in his life to save him. As he
dwells on God as his Savior, he is moved to worship
and praise. He had not yet received the deliverance
he cried out for; he was still waiting. But his heart
had turned toward God in worship, anticipating the
deliverance God would bring.

John Calvin says this about the psalmist's response
in Psalm 13:

> The psalmist does not as yet feel how much he has
> profited by praying; but depending upon the hope
> of deliverance, which the faithful promise of God
> enabled him to entertain, he makes use of this hope
> as a shield to repel those temptations with the terror
> of which he might be greatly distressed. Although,
> therefore, he is severely afflicted, and a multiplicity

of cares urge him to despair, he, notwithstanding, declares it to be his resolution to continue firm in his reliance upon the grace of God, and in the hope of salvation … David, it is true, had not yet obtained what he earnestly desired, but being fully convinced that God was already at hand to grant him deliverance, he pledges himself to give thanks to him for it. And surely it becomes us to engage in prayer in such a frame of mind as at the same time to be ready to sing the praises of God; a thing which is impossible, unless we are fully persuaded that our prayers will not be ineffectual. We may not be wholly free from sorrow, but it is nevertheless necessary that this cheerfulness of faith rise above it, and put into our mouth a song on account of the joy which is reserved for us in the future although not as yet experienced by us.[3]

Doing the Hard Work

This step of the laments involves some hard work. It involves an exercise of faith. It requires forward movement and action. As we just read regarding Psalm 13, the psalmist had to do the hard work of trusting God before he experienced the deliverance he sought.

Recently, my son asked me, 'Mom, when I pray for God to help me, do I just wait for Him to help me or do I need to do something too?' Good question!

I responded, 'Both.'

I read to him this passage from Philippians: 'Therefore, my beloved, as you have always obeyed,

---

3.   Calvin, John. *Commentary on the Psalms*. Kindle Edition, Location: 91499-91528.

so now, not only as in my presence but now much more in my absence, work out your own salvation with fear and trembling, for it is God who works in you, both to will and to work for his good pleasure' (Phil. 2:12-13).

There is a tension in Scripture that seems contradictory but it is not. We know that we are saved by grace. We know that we are completely dependent upon God's grace for all things. We know that we cannot change on our own and that we need God to do the work in us. But there is a tension because God's Word also says that we are responsible to 'work out our salvation with fear and trembling.' We are to run the race (Heb. 12:1) and fight the good fight of faith (1 Tim. 6:12). God calls us to a life of obedience and to do the hard work of trusting and living out our faith.

The fact is, both things are true. Spurgeon said this about reconciling the tension between God's sovereign control and our responsibility, 'I never reconcile two friends, never.'[4] Jerry Bridges in his book *Respectable Sins* puts it this way:

> There is a fundamental principle of the Christian life that I call the principle of *dependent responsibility*; that is, we are responsible before God to obey His Word, to put to death the sins in our lives, both the so-called acceptable sins and the obviously not acceptable ones. At the same time, we do not have the ability within ourselves to carry out this responsibility. We are in fact totally dependent

---

4. Spurgeon, Charles. *Jacob and Esau:* Sermon No. 241, http://www.spurgeon.org/sermons/0239.htm, (accessed April 7, 2015).

upon the enabling power of the Holy Spirit. In this sense, we are both responsible and dependent.[5]

He also says, 'Here the wisdom of some of the older writers will help us: "Work as it if all depends on you, and yet trust as if you did not work at all."'[6]

When it comes to our emotions and the ways in which we are held captive and led by our emotions, we have to put some hard work into this process of gaining freedom from that captivity. Yes, God is at work. Yes, He is the One who 'works in you, both to will and to work for his good pleasure'(Phil. 2:13). But He also calls us to obedience. And this is the place in our journey where we have to work hard at trusting God, we have to exercise our faith, weed out sin, go beneath the layers of our emotions to find the truth, and respond to God in praise and worship for who He is and what He has done.

Though we have been given work to do, it is not ultimately our work, but God's work. He gives us responsibilities and calls us to trust and obey but even the work we do is a gift of His grace. We've been given His Holy Spirit who lives within us. He convicts, encourages, guides, comforts, teaches, and directs us. And even when we can't do the hard work, He is still at work within us. In fact, He is always at work. Even in our darkest days, the Spirit never ceases His work in us. This is a glorious truth that all believers need to carry in their heart.

5.   Bridges, Jerry. *Respectable Sins: Confronting the Sins We Tolerate* (Colorado Springs, CO: NavPress, 2007), p. 41.

6.   Ibid., p. 49.

Nothing that we experience, no tear that we shed, no pain that we endure, no sin that we commit, gets wasted in God's economy. He uses it all to change us into the likeness of His Son. 'And we all, with unveiled face, beholding the glory of the Lord, are being transformed into the same image from one degree of glory to another. For this comes from the Lord who is the Spirit' (2 Cor. 3:18). In His grace, God has guaranteed that the work He began in us, He will finish, 'And I am sure of this, that he who began a good work in you will bring it to completion at the day of Jesus Christ' (Phil. 1:6).

This step of the laments is the part where many of us get to and we stop. It's easy to cry out to God and ask for help but to trust Him in the darkness where we cannot see what's ahead of us? That's the hard part. It's also hard to worship Him when our hearts are breaking, when our feelings tell us that we've been abandoned and that there is no hope left. But I don't want you to give up. We will look at a few practical steps and specific things to do in later chapters. Until then, pray for strength and endurance in this process. Don't give up. Don't turn to distractions or other things to numb you to what's happening. Cling to this promise from the prophet, 'You will seek me and find me, when you seek me with all your heart' (Jer. 29:13).

Where the Mind and Heart Meet

In this step of the laments, we see the psalmist applying what he knows to be true about God to his heart. Here is where the mind and heart meet. This is where the truths in Scripture that we know in our mind intersect with our hearts and reshape our emotions to conform to the truth. Often we allow our emotions to lead us and take precedence over our minds. The laments show us that both the mind and heart can meet together. They show us that the truth of God's Word we have stored in our minds can lead the heart to rejoice in that truth. This is what David did in Psalm 13. He knew God was his Savior and that He is a God of love. This truth in his mind moved his heart out of a place of despair and into a place of trust and worship. That is the trajectory we are following in the laments. We are moving forward from despair to joy and fear to trust.

As Jen Wilkin wrote, in her book, *Women of the Word*, 'The heart cannot love what the mind does not know … the path to transformation runs from the mind to the heart, and not the other way around.'[7] This is where our theology and what we know about God from His Word comes in. The word theology means the study of God. What we learn about God in Scripture, about who He is, what He has done, and who we are in light of all that is the foundation to our faith. It is an anchor that holds us when the storms of life blow into our lives. It is a light that guides us and directs us in the darkness of our circumstances. When our emotions are taking us on a roller coaster ride, our theology is the steady horizon that keeps us in place.

Here are just a few examples of how theology can inform and guide your emotions:

---

7. Wilkin, Jen. *Women of the Word: How to Study the Bible With Both Our Hearts and Our Minds* (Chicago, IL: Crossway, 2014), p. 31.

When your heart is filled with fear because your child is sick and the doctors don't know why and they order more and more tests, it's your theology that tells you that God is in sovereign control of all things. It tells you that God is not surprised by what is happening, nor is He at a loss as to what to do. Your theology reminds you that everything is under His control and that He is working all things out for your good and His glory.

When you are so weary and worn and your husband tells you he has to work out of town for a week and your heart drops in despair, it is your theology that tells you that God will provide you with the grace you need for every moment. It is your theology that reminds you that you can't do life on your own and that without Christ, you can do nothing. It tells you that your rest and hope are found in Christ alone and that you can trust Him to sustain you.

When you've experienced a loss so painful that it feels as though a part of you has been severed, it is your theology that tells you that your Savior also knows grief and sorrow. Your theology reminds you that the pains and horrors of this life are the result of the fall in the Garden and that the suffering we endure mattered so much to God that He did something about it. He entered this world, taking on the same frail flesh we wear, and endured more pain and sorrow than we could ever imagine. Your theology reminds you that He knows that pain you feel, for He too was cut off from whom He loved most when the Father turned His back on Him at the cross. The separation He endured as He bore the weight of our sins secured our redemption and freedom. And one day, He will return to end the world of sin and sorrow once and for all.

The fact is, our emotions are not always trustworthy. They often lead us down dark paths that are hard to turn back from. But they do tell us something is wrong. They are warning signs that we ought to heed. As we have learned so far in our journey, we need to take those emotions to the throne of grace. And as we stand before the throne, we need to do what the laments teach us: to focus on God and His Word. We need to let God's Word and the truth about who He is guide our hearts and reshape our emotions so that, like the psalmist, we can respond in trust and worship.

When Joy Co-mingles

There are two Psalms of Lament that do not end in a response of trust and worship: Psalms 44 and 88. Psalm 44 does not end with a restoration of trust, only a plea for help. 'Why do you hide your face? Why do you forget our affliction and oppression? For our soul is bowed down to the dust; our belly clings to the ground. Rise up; come to our help! Redeem us for the sake of your steadfast love!' (vv. 24-26). Psalm 88 ends with the saddest and darkest note of all the songs, 'Your wrath has swept over me; your dreadful assaults destroy me. They surround me like a flood all day long; they close in on me together. You have caused my beloved and my friend to shun me; my companions have become darkness' (vv. 16-18).

There are times when our emotions are so painful that all we can do is cry out to God. All we can do is ask for His help. Though Psalm 88 does not end on a positive note, it still affirms God as Savior, 'O Lord, God of my salvation; I cry out day and night before you' (v. 1). When our own laments struggle to respond in worship, we have to rest in the fact that Jesus is interceding for us and that the Holy Spirit is crying out on our behalf. Jesus' perfect obedience covers even our weakness of faith. Praise God that it is not the strength of our faith which saves us but the object of our faith, Jesus Christ!

There may also be times when we go through this journey with the psalmist and we respond in trust and worship and still feel grief. We may still feel intense sorrow. This process of following the structure of the laments is not a magical incantation that erases all our emotions. It's not a step by step list to follow that will take away our problems. But it is a journey that draws us closer to God.

This journey may take a long time. It may be one that is repeated over and over. As long as we live in this fallen world, we will have to bear hard emotions. Those visitors I mentioned before will come for a return visit even after we've asked them to leave. Though we follow the example of the psalmist and turn to God with our emotions, crying out for His help, some of those emotions might remain around for a while.

But the good news is that they don't linger alone; joy can be there as well. The joy that we find in the laments, the joy that comes from trusting in God, the joy that bubbles over into praise and worship is what I like to call gospel joy. Gospel joy is what accompanies the gift of faith. It is a fruit, the product of the Holy Spirit who lives within all the redeemed (Gal. 5:22). It is the deep foundational joy that comes from knowing God and being known by God. It is the joy of knowing that we are no longer separated from our Creator but have been redeemed and restored into right relationship with Him through Christ's life, death, and resurrection. And this gospel joy only grows the more we realize the depths and riches of Christ's love for us.

This joy can co-mingle with other emotions. It can co-exist side by side with other feelings and circumstances like sorrow and fear. Even when life is at its hardest, gospel joy is still there. It is always present, like an anchor in the storms of life. It's what trickles through the cracks of our messy and sin-stained lives. Like a river's current, it carries us through the challenges and pains of life in this fallen world. This is why fellow believers in Christ whom we know are going through a serious trial in their lives can still express their joy in the Lord. Even though their world is crumbling, even though they might be facing excruciating physical pains, they can still sing a song of praise because they have gospel joy co-mingling with their sorrow and grief. They can sing because Christ has set them free from all captivity, including captivity to their emotions. They aren't held hostage by their emotions so that even through tears, they can sing of God's amazing grace.

This gospel joy is why the hymn writer, Horatio Spafford could pen the song 'It is Well With My Soul' after losing four of his daughters at sea:

When peace, like a river, attendeth my way,
When sorrows like sea billows roll;
Whatever my lot, Thou hast taught me to say,
It is well, it is well with my soul.

It is well with my soul,
It is well, it is well with my soul.

Though Satan should buffet, though trials should come,
Let this blest assurance control,
That Christ hath regarded my helpless estate,
And hath shed His own blood for my soul.

Though sorrows, fears, and pains remain in this life and though they will revisit us throughout the course of our lives, we have the constant undercurrent of joy always there with us. Though painful emotions are part of the reality of life, they do not have to rule over us. I don't want you to get to the end of this book and think that you will now live a life free of any painful emotions if you just follow the structure of the laments. Rather, I want you to know wherein lies your hope and in whom lie your joy and salvation. It is that truth that will give you gospel joy no matter the circumstances and sorrows of your life. For as Jesus told His disciples, 'I have said these things to you, that in me you may have peace. In the world you will have tribulation. But take heart; I have overcome the world' (John 16:33).

For Your Heart

1. Select one of the following Psalms of Lament and read through it, seeking the three-part structure we have learned so far: 3, 6, 17, 22, 59, 69, 71, 79, 86, 102, 142.

2. How does the psalm you selected speak of Christ? How might it be fulfilled through Christ?

3. Does the psalm speak of God's love and His salvation?

4. Do you hesitate to do the hard work spoken of in this chapter? Why or why not?

5. Do you understand the need for your theology to help shape your emotions? What areas of God's Word are you weak in?

6. Do you think it's possible for joy to co-mingle with other emotions? How have you seen this in your own life or in the life of others? Pray for greater gospel joy.

PART 3

More
from
the Laments

9

Remembering God's Faithfulness

A few years ago I was in the midst of depression and I was scared. The memories of my last visit from Despair were fresh and vivid. I remembered the dark place it had brought me to before and I was terrified to return to that place. And so when Despair visited me again, I was fearful and on edge, knowing that a deep pit awaited me around the next corner. With one last shred of hope, I reached out to my pastor, seeking his wisdom and counsel.

And there in that office as I sobbed and asked him what I should do, he said to me something that I'll never forget. He said that he heard me tell him about all the things I had tried to do to make Despair go away. He heard my list of coping skills, of trying to change my life's circumstances, and of relying on external solutions. 'But I haven't heard you tell me how you are trusting in what Christ already did for you.' When he said those words I thought, 'Well of course I know what Christ did for me, but what does that have to do with my depression? How is that going to help shut off this valve of tears?'

We went on to talk about what it means that Christ lived a perfect life for me, died for me, and rose from the grave for me. My pastor reminded me of the gospel and how it applies to all areas of my life. While I didn't leave the office that day completely transformed with a heart as light and carefree as Pollyanna, I did leave with a new seed of hope. As the months went on, that hope grew and grew as I learned to focus on God's faithfulness for me in Christ.

Remembering the Past

Have you ever gathered with old college friends or maybe friends you grew up with and reminisced about days past? When I get together with old friends someone always starts by saying, 'Remember when …' and then we all go around sharing favorite stories. We tease each other about embarrassing things we once did. We laugh about the immature decisions we made. We tell the same jokes and the same stories we've heard over and over. It's a joy to reminisce with old friends about the past.

Looking back to the past can be both a hindrance and a help. When the past controls us, through guilt or shame, it is a hindrance. When the past haunts us or defines us or points a finger at us, it's not a help. Other times, looking to the past can be fun as we recall and laugh at joyful times. Historians tell us that looking to the past can help us learn from the lessons of others so that we don't make the same mistakes. Looking back to the past is important and helpful to us spiritually when we need a reminder of God's grace and faithfulness toward us.

How Scripture Remembers the Past

Scripture is full of admonitions to remember the past. In the Old Testament, the Israelites celebrated various feasts during the year to remember all that God had done for them. Parents were instructed to repeatedly tell their children the story of their redemption from slavery. Many events in Israel's history were marked with pillars and monuments to remember what happened at a specific location. Israel's prophets, priests, and kings also reminded the people of what God had done for them in rescuing them from slavery and bringing them to the Promised Land.

One way the Israelites remembered the ways God had performed amazing miracles on their behalf was by creating physical markers or memorials. After

Joshua led them through the Jordan River, God said to Joshua, 'Take twelve men from the people, from each tribe a man, and command them, saying, "Take twelve stones from here out of the midst of the Jordan, from the very place where the priests' feet stood firmly, and bring them over with you and lay them down in the place where you lodge tonight." Then Joshua called the twelve men from the people of Israel, whom he had appointed, a man from each tribe. And Joshua said to them,"Pass on before the ark of the Lord your God into the midst of the Jordan, and take up each of you a stone upon his shoulder, according to the number of the tribes of the people of Israel, that this may be a sign among you. When your children ask in time to come, 'What do those stones mean to you?' then you shall tell them that the waters of the Jordan were cut off before the ark of the covenant of the Lord. When it passed over the Jordan, the waters of the Jordan were cut off. So these stones shall be to the people of Israel a memorial forever"' (Josh. 4:1-7).

The Israelites also remembered what God had done for them through their feasts and special holidays. One such special day was that of Passover, a celebration instituted by God on the night when He delivered them from the last and final plague:

> The Lord said to Moses and Aaron in the land of Egypt, 'This month shall be for you the beginning of months. It shall be the first month of the year for you. Tell all the congregation of Israel that on the tenth day of this month every man shall take

a lamb according to their fathers' houses, a lamb for a household ... Then they shall take some of the blood and put it on the two doorposts and the lintel of the houses in which they eat it. They shall eat the flesh that night, roasted on the fire; with unleavened bread and bitter herbs they shall eat it. Do not eat any of it raw or boiled in water, but roasted, its head with its legs and its inner parts. And you shall let none of it remain until the morning; anything that remains until the morning you shall burn. In this manner you shall eat it: with your belt fastened, your sandals on your feet, and your staff in your hand. And you shall eat it in haste. It is the LORD's Passover ... This day shall be for you a memorial day, and you shall keep it as a feast to the LORD; throughout your generations, as a statute forever, you shall keep it as a feast' (Exod. 12:1-3, 7-11, 14).

The prophet Jeremiah cried out to God in prayer when he was in despair over the looming destruction of God's people. As he prayed, he looked behind to the past and remembered God's faithfulness.

You have shown signs and wonders in the land of Egypt, and to this day in Israel and among all mankind, and have made a name for yourself, as at this day. You brought your people Israel out of the land of Egypt with signs and wonders, with a strong hand and outstretched arm, and with great terror. And you gave them this land, which you swore to their fathers to give them, a land flowing with milk and honey. (Jer. 32:20-22)

The New Testament also speaks about the import-ance of remembering the past, particularly our own exodus event, Christ's sacrifice for our sins. Our Lord Himself, on the night He was betrayed, instituted the Lord's Supper as a time for us to remember and reflect on what He has done for us at the cross. 'And he took bread, and when he had given thanks, he broke it and gave it to them, saying, "This is my body, which is given for you. Do this in remembrance of me" ' (Luke 22:19). Paul pointed back to the gospel to remind the Galatians of their freedom in Christ (Gal. 3). Peter pointed out that failing to remember the gospel and what Christ did for us can make us fruitless in our lives (2 Pet. 1:3-9).

The Psalms and the Past

Remembering God's faithfulness toward us in the past is another element we see in some of the laments. For the writers during the time of the Psalms, the two main events they looked back to were the Exodus, their focal salvation event, and God's establishment of David's kingly throne. Reading these laments teaches us that remembrance is important for our own heart, especially as we experience difficult and painful emotions. When God seems silent and winter lingers in our heart far too long, remembering God's steadfast faithfulness for us in Christ, gives us confidence in what He will do in the present and in the future.

One such example is found in Psalm 77 where the writer was in despair. 'I cry aloud to God, aloud to God, and he will hear me' (v. 1). He felt as though God had left him and abandoned him. He wondered if he would ever hear from God again. Then he turned his heart to what God had done in the past,

I will remember the deeds of the LORD; yes, I will remember your wonders of old. I will ponder all your work, and meditate on your mighty deeds. Your way, O God, is holy. What god is great like our God? You are the God who works wonders; you have made known your might among the peoples. You with your arm redeemed your people, the children of Jacob and Joseph. When the waters saw you, O God, when the waters saw you, they were afraid; indeed, the deep trembled. The clouds poured out water; the skies gave forth thunder; your arrows flashed on every side. The crash of your thunder was in the whirlwind; your lightnings lighted up the world; the earth trembled and shook. Your way was through the sea, your path through the great waters; yet your footprints were unseen. You led your people like a flock by the hand of Moses and Aaron. (vv. 11-20)

The Gospel Transformation Study Bible says this about this passage, 'In times of soul disturbance, we must seek God … After he unloads his heart, Asaph begins to calm down and submit his will to the Lord. By doing so, a believer will gain a more patient perspective on God's future redemptive plans (2 Pet. 3:9, James 5:11). Remembering God's past deeds will also build confidence in God's justice by revealing three of God's attributes: his holiness (Ps. 77:13), greatness (vv. 13-14), and care (v. 15). These attributes of the Lord are finally given flesh-and-blood reality in Jesus of Nazareth. Asaph's final comfort is that God "led [his] people like a flock by the hand of Moses and Aaron" (v. 20). How did the Lord do this? "Your way was through the sea" (v. 19). This is an allusion to the exodus, when God opened the Red Sea to deliver his people. Then as now, God performs miracles to deliver his beloved people—the greatest miracle of all being the incarnation, life, death, and resurrection of the Son of God, for sinners such as us.[1]

John Calvin says this about Psalm 77, 'the wonderful power of God which he has always put forth for the preservation and salvation of his servants, provided we duly reflect upon it, is sufficient to enable us to overcome all sorrows.'[2] This is what happened to me after I met with my pastor; I learned to reflect on the gospel, to dwell on, meditate on, and saturate my heart with what Christ had done for me and in so doing, it moved me out of a state of despair and into a place of hope and trust.

A few other laments show the psalmist remembering God's redemptive work in the past:

> I remember the days of old; I meditate on all that you have done; I ponder the work of your hands. (Ps. 143:5)

> Yet God my King is from of old, working salvation in the midst of the earth. You divided the sea by your might; you broke the heads of the sea monsters on the waters. You crushed the heads of Leviathan; you gave him as food for the creatures of the wilderness. You split open springs and brooks; you dried up ever-flowing streams. Yours is the day, yours also the night; you have established the

---

1. *Gospel Transformation Bible*, pp. 723-4.
2. Calvin, John. *Commentary on the Psalms*. Kindle Location: 116001.

heavenly lights and the sun. You have fixed all the boundaries of the earth; you have made summer and winter. (Ps. 74:12-17)

My God, my God, why have you forsaken me? Why are you so far from saving me, from the words of my groaning? O my God, I cry by day, but you do not answer, and by night, but I find no rest. Yet you are holy, enthroned on the praises of Israel. In you our fathers trusted; they trusted, and you delivered them. To you they cried and were rescued; in you they trusted and were not put to shame. (Ps. 22:1-5)

Remembering God's Faithfulness in Redemptive History

As believers living on this side of redemptive history, we have God's complete Word. We have the entire Bible, which shows us from beginning to end God's steadfast faithfulness. We can look to the promise of the Redeemer in Genesis 3:15 and see its fulfillment take place in the Gospels. We can see that God is a covenant-keeping God who fulfills His promises to His people. We have the testimony of the New Testament writers from which to see God's beautiful plan of redemption come to fruition in the life, death, and resurrection of Jesus Christ.

One of the ways we can remember and dwell on God's faithfulness toward us is to review and remember the story of Creation, Fall, Redemption, and Restoration. This is the story I review in my own heart on a regular basis.

When life is hard and painful and the tears flow freely, we can look back to the story of Creation to remember God's original plan. The pains of this life that we experience were not part of that original creation. The reason we struggle so much with the injustices and heartaches of this world is because deep down we know it's not supposed to be this way.

When our hearts cry out 'Why?' because we've been hurt by loved ones or experienced a loss or everything we've worked for has been ripped away from us, we can remember the story of the fall. When Adam and Eve fell into sin, all mankind fell with them. Sin has affected the entire world bringing forth illness, natural disaster, accidents, as well as the sins we see committed all around us every day. Sin has saturated our entire being such that not only do we commit sins, we **are** sinners. And so is everyone else. But God promised a Rescuer and He confirmed His promise throughout the Old Testament.

We must then continue to follow what God has done and focus our heart on the gospel, the story of redemption. This is that key of promise I mentioned at the beginning of the book. Just as the Israelites looked back to their exodus from slavery as evidence of God's faithful love toward them, we can look back to our exodus from sin. We can remember the cross and what Christ did for us in taking the punishment we deserve. In dwelling on our own exodus, we remember that Christ brought us from death to life. We remember that the redemption He purchased restored our relationship with God, giving us complete and full access to our Father. What Christ did for us, through His perfect life and sacrificial death, is the greatest act of grace. Remembering this grace strengthens us in the present and gives us courage for the future, not in ourselves and what we can do, but in God and in what He has done and will continue to do.

As Dietrich Bonhoeffer wrote, 'Because God's word has spoken to us in history and thus in the past, the remembrance and repetition of what we have learned is a necessary daily exercise. Every day we must turn again to God's acts of salvation, so that we can again move forward ... Faith and obedience live on remembrance and repetition. Remembrance becomes the power of the present because of the living God who once acted for me and who reminds me of that today.'[3]

Not only that, but the story isn't over. We have hope for eternity because of what Christ has done. Jesus said He is making all things new and one day He will return to judge the earth and gather His people together from every corner of the earth. Sin will be conquered once and for all. We can look forward to the day when, 'He will wipe away every tear from their eyes, and death shall be no more, neither shall there be mourning, nor crying, nor pain anymore, for the former things have passed away' (Rev. 21:4).

Remembering His Faithfulness in Our Everyday Lives

In addition to God's great grace and faithfulness for us at the cross, there are countless daily acts of grace He gives us in our lives. God pours out His riches for us every day in ways we can't fathom.

---

3. Bonhoeffer, Dietrich. *I Want to Live These Days With You: A Year of Daily Devotions* (Louisville, KY: Westminster, John Knox Press, 2007), p. 15.

John Piper once wrote, 'God is always doing 10,000 things in your life, and you may be aware of three of them.'[4] Looking back at the ways He has provided food when we needed, the ways He has comforted us when we've been in sorrow, the ways He has supplied us with wisdom when we had none, these are all acts of grace we can reflect on when we need a reminder of His faithfulness.

Whenever money has been in short supply, I always remind myself of the early days of our marriage when God miraculously provided for us and I rest in the confidence that God is always faithful to provide. Whenever I've worried about what I should do next, when God's will seems unclear and I feel so uncertain, I remember times in the past when I've felt the same and I remember how God brought me through those times, guiding and directing me. When I fear the worst, I remember God's grace and comfort all the other times I've been afraid.

We need to be watchful and look for the ways God moves in our lives. Nothing happens by accident. I often pray that God would help me to see all the little details that He takes care of for me. I don't want to miss a single thing that He is doing so that I can praise Him for it. These 10,000 things are a testimony of God's faithfulness toward us. In both the big and small, God is always faithful.

---

4.   Piper, John. 'Every Moment in 2013 God Will Be Doing 10,000 Things in Your Life,' January 1, 2013, http://www.desiringgod. org/articles/every-moment-in-2013-god-will-be-doing-10-000- things-in-your-life (accessed February 25, 2015).

There are many worries and fears in this life. There are so many heartaches and sorrows and tears. Our focus is often pulled on to the trials at hand in the present. Sometimes our minds are pushed into the future, considering all the things that could go wrong. That's when we need to look back to the past, where God has shown His love and grace for us at the cross. Like the stones that Joshua laid on the other side of the river Jordan, the cross stands as a testimony for all time that God can deliver us from our greatest fear, the greatest evil, and the greatest obstacle of our life. Like the writers in the Psalms, when the cares of this life weigh us down, we need to look back and remember God's faithfulness. For it gives us confidence and assurance that He will sustain us in the present and carry us into the future.

For Your Heart

1. Read Psalms 74 and 77. What specific characteristics or actions of God does the psalmist focus on?

2. How does looking to God's work in your life in the past, both in the big things (salvation) and in the small day to day things, give you confidence in His ongoing faithfulness in your life?

3. What specific things can you think of that He has done? Take time to pray about those things and express your gratitude for His faithful work in your life.

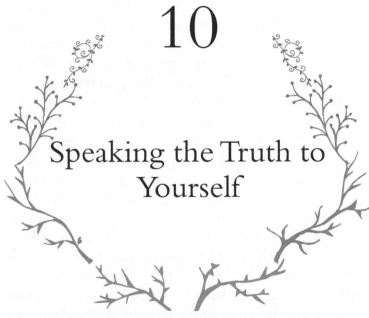

10

Speaking the Truth to Yourself

I woke up that morning sick. I felt feverish, my head hurt, and the world seemed to be spinning a little too fast. 'I'll never make it to the end of the day,' I muttered to myself. My husband was due to leave town for work and would be gone a couple of days. 'How am I going to manage the kids while feeling like this?' These thoughts traveled with me throughout the day, spawning new ones. 'This is too much, I just can't do it.' 'Can't they see that I am sick? Why can't they listen for once?' Before I knew it, I was overwhelmed, stressed, irritable, and distraught.

Talking to Ourselves

As a teen, I remember teasing my mother for talking out loud to herself. Now I find myself doing the same thing. While most of us may not be in the habit of talking out loud to ourselves, we do keep a constant internal dialogue going with ourselves. We think and chatter on to ourselves all day. For example, when we carry on a conversation with someone, even while we are talking to them, we are thinking about that person and making comments to ourselves about them. When we see someone doing something, we make judgment calls about them; we assume and presuppose their motivations, making inferences about their behavior. When we face a challenge in our day, we talk about the challenge with ourselves. We determine whether it's a challenge we can handle, make decisions about how to face the challenge, and encourage or discourage ourselves in the process. All of this happens in the quietness inside our mind. On that day when I was sick, my internal dialogue told me that the challenge was too hard, that I wouldn't make it through, and that life was too overwhelming.

Our thoughts carry great weight in our lives. They determine our emotions and our behavior. They are like the rudder that steers a boat. As Jesus said, 'For out of the abundance of the heart the mouth speaks' (Matt. 12:34). Solomon warned his sons, 'Keep your heart with all vigilance, for from it flow the springs of life' (Prov. 4:23). This is why David said, 'I have stored up your word in my heart, that I might not sin against you' (Ps. 119:11).

When it comes to our thoughts and the dialogue we have with ourselves, the problem is, we all too often fail to talk back to ourselves. Instead, we listen to ourselves and agree with what we are saying rather than speak the truth back to ourselves. The late Dr. Martyn Lloyd-Jones put it like this, 'Have you realized that most of your unhappiness in life is due to the fact that you are listening to yourself instead of talking to yourself? Take those thoughts that come to you the moment you wake up in the morning. You have not originated them, but they start talking to you, they bring back the problems of yesterday, etc. Somebody is talking. Who is talking to you? Your self is talking to you.'[1]

Talking Back to Ourselves

Another one of the lessons we can glean from the Psalms of Lament is the way the psalmist talks back to himself. While he verbalizes what he is thinking and feeling, no matter how dark those thoughts and feelings are, he doesn't stay there in the place of catharsis. This is a crucial truth for us to learn from the Psalms of Lament. These heart cries follow a forward movement. They don't simply express emotions and leave it at that, because though verbalizing what we are feeling does provide some relief, it's not our

1.   Lloyd-Jones, D. Martyn. *Spiritual Depression: Its Causes and Its Cure* (Grand Rapids, MI: Wm. B. Eerdmans, 1965), pp. 20, 21.

ultimate destination. As we learned in previous chapters, we are ultimately moving toward a place of trust and worship. Learning to speak the truth back to ourselves, as the psalmist does, helps move us toward our journey's end.

A great example of this is seen in Psalm 42. This Psalm of Lament was written by the Sons of Korah. It is a psalm that laments God's absence. The author had to be away from Jerusalem, the place where God's dwelling place was. He was also feeling the presence of his enemies and cried out to God for help.

'As a deer pants for flowing streams, so pants my soul for you, O God. My soul thirsts for God, for the living God. When shall I come and appear before God? My tears have been my food day and night, while they say to me all the day long, "Where is your God?"'(vv. 1-3). He goes on to talk to himself, to confront his despair saying, 'Why are you cast down, O my soul, and why are you in turmoil within me? Hope in God; for I shall again praise him, my salvation'(v. 5). In this psalm, the writer challenges and confronts himself with the truth. He talks back to himself, reminding himself that his hope is in God and that God is his Savior.

In Psalm 27, David is surrounded by his enemies. He is on the run for his life. He also speaks the truth to himself. He tells his fears, 'The LORD is my light and my salvation; whom shall I fear? The LORD is the stronghold of my life; of whom shall I be afraid? When evildoers assail me to eat up my flesh, my adversaries and foes, it is they who stumble and fall.

Though an army encamp against me, my heart shall not fear; though war arise against me, yet I will be confident' (vv. 1-3). He stood his ground against his fears, trusting in the God of his salvation.

David laments a betrayal by a friend in Psalm 55. It was a real betrayal experienced by David, but one that also anticipates the betrayal Jesus experienced by Judas. It was a painful betrayal for David because it was by someone with whom he had gone and worshipped the Lord. 'But it is you, a man, my equal, my companion, my familiar friend. We used to take sweet counsel together; within God's house we walked in the throng' (vv. 13-14). His heart ached over the betrayal. 'My thoughts trouble me and I am distraught ... My heart is in anguish within me; the terrors of death assail me. Fear and trembling have beset me; horror has overwhelmed me' (vv. 2-4). David then tells himself the truth, 'Cast your cares on the Lord and he will sustain you' (v. 22).

In 2 Corinthians 10:5, the Apostle Paul talks about taking 'every thought captive to obey Christ'. When we feel overwhelmed, stressed, worried, anxious, fearful, and in despair, we need to talk back to ourselves. We can't be lazy thinkers. We need to take charge of our thoughts, not allowing them to wander down rabbit trails. We need to speak back to ourselves the truth of God's Word. Like the writers of Psalm 27, 42, and 55, we need to point ourselves to the hope we have in God through Jesus Christ.

As Dr. Lloyd-Jones wrote, 'You have to take yourself in hand, you have to address yourself, preach to yourself, question yourself. You must say to your soul: "Why art thou cast down—what business have you to be disquieted?" You must turn on yourself, upbraid yourself, condemn yourself, exhort yourself, and say to yourself: "Hope thou in God" – instead of muttering in this depressed, unhappy way. And then you must go on to remind yourself of God, Who God is, and what God is and what God has done, and what God has pledged Himself to do.'[2]

Speaking the Truth

Too often our emotions tell us half-truths and sometimes even downright lies. Our emotions can exaggerate our circumstances to the point that we feel like our entire world has been flipped upside down. Like a thick layer of morning fog, our emotions can also cloud and distort the truth so that we can't even see it. When we feel emotions like fear, sorrow, despair, abandonment, or worry, we need to be prepared to draw from the deep wells of God's Word, saturating our heart with His truth. We need to compare what we are telling ourselves with what God's Word says.

We do this because God's Word is the source of all truth. It is our ultimate authority. It is our source of all wisdom and knowledge. God's Word sanctifies, transforms, and divides truth from fiction. 'Sanctify them in the truth; your word is truth' (John 17:17). 'For the word of God is living and active, sharper than any two-edged sword, piercing to the division of soul and of spirit, of joints and of marrow, and discerning

---

2. Lloyd-Jones, D. Martyn. *Spiritual Depression: Its Causes and Its Cure*, p. 21.

the thoughts and intentions of the heart' (Heb. 4:12). 'Forever, O Lᴏʀᴅ, your word is firmly fixed in the heavens … Your righteousness is righteous forever, and your law is true' (Ps. 119:89, 142).

This means we need to be intentional and diligent in the kinds of thoughts we think. Paul says in Philippians 4:8, 'Whatever is true, whatever is honorable, whatever is just, whatever is pure, whatever is lovely, whatever is commendable, if there is any excellence, if there is anything worthy of praise, think about these things.' These are the thoughts we need in our minds and the ones we want to foster, take root, and grow.

John Piper points out in his book, *A Godward Life*, that the Bible speaks of an aggressive, non-passive approach to change, that of 'set your mind.' 'Set your mind on the things above, not on the things that are on earth' (Col. 3:2). 'Those who live according to the flesh set their minds on the things of the flesh' (Rom. 8:5). He wrote, 'Our emotions are governed in large measure by what we "consider" — what we dwell on with our minds. For example, Jesus told us to overcome the emotion of anxiety by what we consider. "Do not be anxious … Consider the ravens … Consider the lilies" (Luke 12:22, 24, 27, ʀsv). The mind is the window of the heart. If we let our minds constantly dwell on the dark, the heart will feel dark. If we open the window of our mind to the light, the heart will feel the light … Above all, this great capacity of our minds to focus and consider is meant for considering Jesus: "Holy brethren, partakers of a heavenly calling, consider Jesus … Consider Him who has endured such hostility by sinners against Himself, so that you may not grow weary and lose heart" (Heb. 3:1, 12:3) ... It is when we focus our minds on the glory of Christ that we are transformed from one degree of glory to another (2 Cor. 3:18).'[3]

When we feel overwhelmed by life or fearful of the unknown future or in despair over a trial, what truths from God's Word can we speak to ourselves?

Who we are in Christ
Like Christian on his journey to the Celestial City, we can forget that we have the key of promise. We can forget that the gospel is the key that unlocks us from all our Doubting Castles. Like Christian, we need to remember that we have the key. We need to remember the gospel and who we are because of what Christ has done. We do this by 'preaching the gospel' to ourselves.

Author Jerry Bridges is known for using the term 'preach the gospel.' This means that every day, we remind ourselves of what Christ did for us through His life, death, and resurrection. He writes, 'It is not our contrition or sorrow for our sin, it is not our repentance, it is not even the passing of a certain number of hours during which we feel we are on some kind of probation that cleanses us. It is the blood of Christ, shed once for all on Calvary two thousand years ago but appropriated daily or even many times a day, that cleanses our consciences and gives us a renewed sense of peace with God ... To

3.   Piper, John. *A Godward Life: Savoring the Supremacy of God in all of Life* (Colorado Springs, CO: Multnomah, 1997), p. 229.

preach the gospel to yourself, then means that you continually face up to your own sinfulness and then flee to Jesus through faith in His shed blood and righteous life. It means that you appropriate, again by faith, the fact that Jesus fully satisfied the law of God, that He is your propitiation, and that God's holy wrath is no longer directed toward you. To preach the gospel to yourself means that you take at face value the precious words of Romans 4:7-8: "Blessed are those whose lawless deeds have been forgiven, and whose sins have been covered. Blessed is the man whose sins the Lord will not take into account."[4]

As we preach the gospel to ourselves, remembering what Christ has done, we need to remember who we are because of the gospel. We have been redeemed. We have been changed. This means that God looks at us and sees the righteousness of Christ. 'For our sake he made him to be sin who knew no sin, so that in him we might become the righteousness of God.' (2 Cor. 5:21). And because of the gospel, we are no longer slaves to sin. 'Therefore, if anyone is in Christ, he is a new creation. The old has passed away; behold, the new has come' (2 Cor. 5:17).

We have also been adopted into the family of God; we are sons and daughters of the Most High. 'For you did not receive the spirit of slavery to fall back into fear, but you have received the Spirit of adoption as sons, by whom we cry, "Abba! Father!"'

---

4.   Bridges, Jerry. *The Discipline of Grace: God's Role and Our Role in the Pursuit of Holiness* (Colorado Springs, CO: NavPress, 1994), pp. 58-9.

(Rom. 8:15). As adopted children of God, we are loved as much as the Son (John 17:23). Finally, we are heirs of the Kingdom, 'Blessed be the God and Father of our Lord Jesus Christ! According to his great mercy, he has caused us to be born again to a living hope through the resurrection of Jesus Christ from the dead, to an inheritance that is imperishable, undefiled, and unfading, kept in heaven for you' (1 Pet. 1:3-4).

God's sovereignty
Secondly, we can remind ourselves that God is in sovereign control of all things. Proverbs 21:1 says, 'The king's heart is a stream of water in the hand of the LORD; he turns it wherever he will.' 'Are not two sparrows sold for a penny? And not one of them will fall to the ground apart from your Father' (Matt. 10:29). God holds the world in His hands. Nothing happens outside of His will. In fact, He is not surprised by our circumstances. Nor is He powerless over the circumstances of our lives. 'Who has spoken and it came to pass, unless the Lord has commanded it? Is it not from the mouth of the Most High that good and bad come?' (Lam. 3:37-38). What is happening to us is not by chance. Rather, it is under the control of our sovereign God.

This is a comforting doctrine because it means that nothing is left to chance. 'Whatever the LORD pleases, he does, in heaven and on earth, in the seas and all the deeps' (Ps. 135:6). The circumstances in our lives are not random occurrences. They are all under God's careful direction and watchful eye. 'Behold, he who keeps Israel will neither slumber nor sleep' (Ps. 121:4). 'Have you not known? Have you not heard? The LORD is the everlasting God, the Creator of the ends of the earth. He does not faint or grow weary; his understanding is unsearchable' (Isa. 40:28).

God knows the end from the beginning. He is the author of our story. He is moving that story forward to the great and final chapter where all the questions will be answered and the mysteries revealed. As we live in the middle of the story, we have to trust the author. We have to rest in His sovereign care and believe that He is not out to get us but that He is working all things together for our good.

God's character

Another truth we can tell ourselves is the truth of who God is, His character. He is good, He is holy, and He is just. 'The Rock, his work is perfect, for all his ways are justice. A God of faithfulness and without iniquity, just and upright is he' (Deut. 32:4). He is all-powerful. He is all-knowing. He is faithful. 'For the word of the LORD is upright, and all his work is done in faithfulness' (Ps. 33:4). 'Let us hold fast the confession of our hope without wavering, for he who promised is faithful' (Heb. 10:23). He is gracious, merciful, and kind. 'The LORD is merciful and gracious, slow to anger and abounding in steadfast love' (Ps. 103:8).

We can trust God's intentions for us because of who He is. 'Trust in him at all times, O people; pour out your heart before him; God is a refuge for us' (Ps. 62:8). His character doesn't change. While we and our circumstances change, He remains the same. 'Every good gift and every perfect gift is from above, coming down from the Father of lights with whom there is no variation or shadow due to change' (James 1:17). 'But you are the same, and your years have no end' (Ps. 102:27).

God's promises

Because God is faithful and trustworthy and because He does not change, we can trust and rely on His promises. When everything seems frightening, uncertain, out of control and it seems like everything and everyone is against us, we need to remind ourselves of all God has promised us.

He has promised salvation for everyone who calls on His name. 'All that the Father gives me will come to me, and whoever comes to me I will never cast out' (John 6:37). 'And it shall come to pass that everyone who calls upon the name of the Lord shall be saved' (Acts 2:21).

He is always with us. Even when it doesn't feel like He is there, He is there. 'Have I not commanded you? Be strong and courageous. Do not be frightened, and do not be dismayed, for the Lord your God is with you wherever you go' (Josh. 1:9) 'Fear not, for I am with you; be not dismayed, for I am your God; I will strengthen you, I will help you, I will uphold you with my righteous right hand' (Isa. 41:10). He hears us when we cry out to Him. 'The eyes of the Lord are toward the righteous and his ears toward their cry' (Ps. 34:15). He has also promised to never leave us or forsake us. 'For I am sure that neither death nor life, nor angels nor demons, nor things present nor things to come, nor powers, nor height nor depth, nor anything else in all creation, will be able to separate us from the love of God in Christ Jesus our Lord' (Rom. 8:38-39).

God has also promised to meet all our needs. 'And my God will supply every need of yours according to his riches in glory in Christ Jesus' (Phil. 4:19). And He has promised us eternity with Him in heaven. 'Let not your hearts be troubled. Believe in God; believe also in me. In my Father's house are many rooms. If it were not so, would I have told you that I go to prepare a place for you? And if I go and prepare a place for you, I will come again and will take you to myself, that where I am you may be also' (John 14:1-3).

All these truths from God's Word are anchors for our heart when the waves of circumstances roll over us and when our emotions are tossed to and fro. These are truths we need to imprint upon our heart for the days when life is hard and all seems bleak. Memorize them. Believe them. Trust them.

For Your Heart

1. Read Romans 3:19-26 for an overview of the gospel. Preach it to yourself each day.

2. Write down several of the verses that remind you of who you are because of Christ's work for you on the cross and place them in a prominent place where you will see them often.

3. Read Isaiah 40 and meditate on God's sovereign control of all things. Remind yourself that even now, whatever is going on in your life and heart, God is in control of it, directing it all for His glory and your good.

4. Which of God's promises do you need to cling to right now in your life?

11

The Need
for Confession

As children, one of the first Bible stories we learn
is that of David and Goliath. We sit there with the
other children in Sunday school and listen with
amazement as we imagine what it would have been
like to stand before a giant with just a sling and a few
river stones. David became our hero. We wanted to
be brave and strong like him, trusting God in the
face of evil and fear.

Then as we got older, we learned the story of David and Bathsheba and our hero fell from the pedestal we created for him. We then realized that he was a sinner just like us. While moralistic sermons tend to take David's life and use it as a lesson on how Christians should or should not live their life, there is one thing we can learn from David and that is how to confess our sins.

David's Sin and Confession

Following his adulterous sin with Bathsheba and subsequent murder of her husband, the prophet Nathan confronted David by telling him a story about a rich man stealing a poor man's one and only sheep. David responded to the story with indignation, saying that such a man should be punished. Nathan responded,

> 'You are the man! Thus says the LORD, the God of Israel, "I anointed you king over Israel, and I delivered you out of the hand of Saul. And I gave you your master's house and your master's wives into your arms and gave you the house of Israel and of Judah. And if this were too little, I would add to you as much more. Why have you despised the word of the Lord, to do what is evil in his sight? You have struck down Uriah the Hittite with the sword and have taken his wife to be your wife and have killed him with the sword of the Ammonites. Now therefore the sword shall never depart from your house, because you have despised me and have taken the wife of Uriah the Hittite to be your wife." Thus says the Lord, "Behold, I will raise up evil against you out of your own house. And I will

take your wives before your eyes and give them to your neighbor, and he shall lie with your wives in the sight of this sun. For you did it secretly, but I will do this thing before all Israel and before the sun."' David said to Nathan, 'I have sinned against the LORD.' And Nathan said to David, 'The LORD also has put away your sin; you shall not die. Nevertheless, because by this deed you have utterly scorned the LORD, the child who is born to you shall die'. (2 Sam. 12:7-14)

David was convicted of his sin and wrote this lament in Psalm 51:

Have mercy on me, O God, according to your steadfast love; according to your abundant mercy blot out my transgressions. Wash me thoroughly from my iniquity, and cleanse me from my sin! For I know my transgressions, and my sin is ever before me. Against you, you only, have I sinned and done what is evil in your sight, so that you may be justified in your words and blameless in your judgment. Behold, I was brought forth in iniquity, and in sin did my mother conceive me. Behold, you delight in truth in the inward being, and you teach me wisdom in the secret heart. Purge me with hyssop, and I shall be clean; wash me, and I shall be whiter than snow. Let me hear joy and gladness; let the bones that you have broken rejoice. Hide your face from my sins, and blot out all my iniquities. Create in me a clean heart, O God, and renew a right spirit within me. Cast me not away from your presence, and take not your Holy Spirit from me. Restore to me the joy of your salvation, and uphold me with a willing spirit. Then I will teach

transgressors your ways, and sinners will return
to you. Deliver me from bloodguiltiness, O God,
O God of my salvation, and my tongue will sing
aloud of your righteousness. O Lord, open my
lips, and my mouth will declare your praise. For
you will not delight in sacrifice, or I would give it;
you will not be pleased with a burnt offering. The
sacrifices of God are a broken spirit; a broken and
contrite heart, O God, you will not despise. Do good
to Zion in your good pleasure; build up the walls of
Jerusalem; then will you delight in right sacrifices,
in burnt offerings and whole burnt offerings; then
bulls will be offered on your altar.

After the prophet confronted David with his sin, he
went straight to God in prayer. From our study of the
laments, we can see David's brutal honesty before
God. He cried out for His help and forgiveness. He
relied and trusted in the steadfast love and mercy
of God. He knew that God alone saves and cleanses
from sin. He also knew that his confession was
a sacrifice that God would accept.

Confession in the Laments
As we discussed in Chapter 5, confession is a characteristic of the Psalms of Lament. Though not found
in every lament, where appropriate, the psalmist
confesses his sin.

As sinners, we know that sin plays a huge role
in our daily struggles and pains of life. Sometimes
it is the sins of others against us that bring us grief.
Other times it is the greater effect of sin in the world
through disease and disaster that causes us to have
sorrow. There are also times when our problems

are the direct result of our own sin, as in the case of David's sin against Bathsheba. There are also times when God uses the sin in this world to sanctify us. Sometimes He uses what He hates to bring about something good. We see this most in the story of Job. And then there are times when our troubles are a combination of any and all these factors.

Often, when we are consumed by our emotions, we tend to see only the troubles before us. We think that if only our problems went away, then our life would be better and we'd be happy. We place blame for our pains on our circumstances, on other people, and even on God. We think that if only we had a more attentive husband, bigger house, more children, better job, healthier body, or a safer world then we wouldn't feel so overwhelmed, in despair, or filled with fear.

In focusing so much on the external circumstances, we fail to see the impact of our own sin in our lives. But as the laments teach us, it is important that we include confession of sin in our prayers. As Tremper Longman wrote, 'The psalmist frequently admits his sin to God before turning to him for help. Some Christians neglect this aspect of prayer to their detriment. True, we are forgiven in Christ, but this does not give us license to sin (Rom. 6:1-7)! The sad truth is that we do continue to sin. Thus, we must constantly come before our forgiving Lord in repentance if we expect to grow in our faith. We can learn how to do this by meditating on the laments of the Psalms.'[1]

---

1.   Longman. *How to Read the Psalms*, p. 137.

Sin gets in between us and God. It creates a barrier. This is why Jesus came to redeem us, to bring restoration. David felt that barrier between himself and God and that is why he turned to God in repentance. As Paul Tripp notes, 'Because sin is about the breaking of relationship, restoration of relationship is the only hope for us in our struggle with sin. It's only because God is willing to love us in a way that we refuse to love Him that we have any hope of defeating sin. It's through the gift of adoption into relationship with Him that we find what we need to gain power over sin. And what do we need? A greater love for Him than we have for ourselves. His love for us is the only thing that has the power to produce in us that kind of love for Him. Sin is a relationship, and it takes relationship to deliver us from sin. Christ was willing to experience that rejection that our rebellion deserves so that we could have the relationship with God that's our only hope as we grapple with the selfishness of sin.'[2]

Other laments that contain confession include:

> Remember not the sins of my youth or my transgressions; according to your steadfast love remember me, for the sake of your goodness, O Lord … For your name's sake, O Lord, pardon my guilt, for it is great. (Ps. 25:7, 11)

> O Lord, rebuke me not in your anger, nor discipline me in your wrath! For your arrows have sunk into me, and your hand has come down on me.

---

2.   Tripp, Paul. *Whiter Than Snow: Meditations on Sin and Mercy* (Chicago, IL: Crossway, 2008), p. 82.

There is no soundness in my flesh because of your indignation; there is no health in my bones because of my sin. For my iniquities have gone over my head; like a heavy burden, they are too heavy for me. My wounds stink and fester because of my foolishness. (Ps. 38:1-5)

O God, you know my folly; the wrongs I have done are not hidden from you. Let not those who hope in you be put to shame through me, O Lord God of hosts; let not those who seek you be brought to dishonor through me, O God of Israel. (Ps. 69:5-6)

When the Pain of Conviction Pushes Us to Confession
One of the things we see about the confessions in the laments, particularly from David's lament in Psalm 51, is how the pain of conviction pushes us to confession. One of the Holy Spirit's roles in our lives as believers is to convict us of sin. As painful as that conviction is, it is a good thing.

A couple of years ago, I sinned against a loved one. It was an inconsiderate and thoughtless action on my part and perhaps I could have justified my action away by saying that it wasn't intentional. But God wouldn't let me. He poked and prodded me through the Holy Spirit. He shined a spotlight on my heart so that no matter how hard I tried, I couldn't get away from it. He had me under a microscope. The truth was unavoidable; I am a sinner.

Have you ever walked around all day with food on your face or your hair doing weird things or your clothes stained and you never realized it? Then you finally walk past a mirror and are shocked by how you look. You cringe, realizing everyone else saw you this way but you had no clue. Conviction of sin can be like that in some ways. It's like the Spirit holds up a mirror to our heart and shows us what's really there. The image we had in our minds of ourselves is crushed. We don't have it all together. We are way more sinful than we realized.

When King David sinned against Bathsheba and then had her husband killed in battle, God used the prophet Nathan to point out David's sin to him. He was convicted of his sin and immediately responded, 'I have sinned against the LORD' (2 Sam. 12:13). In David's lament about his sin in Psalm 51, he described how that conviction felt, comparing it to that of broken bones, 'Let the bones that you have broken rejoice' (v. 8b).

I broke my arm one summer while roller-skating with my kids. My skates flew out from underneath me and I landed flat on my back. At first all I felt was embarrassment and soreness in my back where I landed. But before long, my wrist started to hurt. Slowly, over the next hour, the pain worked itself up from my wrist to my elbow. A few hours later I was in agony. I ended up going to the doctor for X-rays and found that I had broken a bone near my elbow. The excruciating pain in my arm was an important pain because it told me that something was wrong.

Sometimes the emotional pain we feel is the result of conviction of sin. The Holy Spirit is doing His work, piercing our hearts. David felt the pressing pain of conviction in Psalm 51. That's why he asked God to restore to him the joy of his salvation and to let the bones He had crushed rejoice. Paul Tripp says in his book, *Whiter Than Snow: Meditations on Sin and Mercy*:

> The physical pain of an actual broken bone is worth being thankful for because it's a warning sign something is wrong in that arm or leg. In the same way, God's loving hammer of conviction is meant to break your heart, and the pain of heart you feel is meant to alert you to the fact that something is spiritually wrong inside of you. Like the warning signal of physical pain, the rescuing and restoring pain of convicting grace is a thing worth celebrating.[3]

Seeing our messy hair or face covered in food particles in the mirror is embarrassing but it's also a good thing because it moves us to fix our hair or clean our face. The pain I felt when I broke my arm was also a good thing, for it made me go to the doctor and get it looked at. And the pressing pain of conviction is an even better thing because it pushes us to the throne of grace where we confess and repent of our sins.

Paul referred to this pain as godly sorrow or what I like to call 'good grief.' 'For even if I made you grieve with my letter, I do not regret it — though I did regret it, for I see that that letter grieved you, though only for a while. As it is, I rejoice, not because you were grieved, but because you were grieved into repenting. For you felt a godly grief, so that you suffered no loss through us. For godly grief produces a repentance that leads to salvation

---

3. Tripp, Paul. *Whiter Than Snow: Meditations on Sin and Mercy* , p. 35.

without regret, whereas worldly grief produces death' (2 Cor. 7:8-10).

This good grief pushes us to repentance where we are then washed anew in the gospel of grace and experience the glory-filled wonder of forgiveness through Jesus Christ. This is what David cried out for in Psalm 51, 'Hide your face from my sins, and blot out all my iniquities. Create in me in a clean heart, O God, and renew a right spirit within me' (vv. 9-10).

Only God can forgive us and take away our sins. In David's time, it occurred through the sacrificial system; in ours, through the perfect and complete sacrifice of Christ on our behalf. The sacrifices David offered on the altar had to be repeated over and over. Hebrews tells us that Christ is the perfect sacrifice, 'For if the blood of goats and bulls, and the sprinkling of defiled persons with the ashes of a heifer, sanctify for the purification of the flesh, how much more will the blood of Christ, who through the eternal Spirit offered himself without blemish to God, purify our conscience from dead works to serve the living God' (Heb. 9:13-14). His death on the cross marked an end to the Old Testament sacrifices and peeled back the curtain that barred us from God's presence. Christ redeemed and restored us back into right relationship to the Father, giving us freedom to come before Him with our good grief in repentance and receive His forgiveness in return. This forgiveness restores our joy, making broken bones (and hearts) rejoice.

Sometimes we have to endure the pain of conviction so that we can face the truth that we are sinners in need of a Savior. Because only then can we experience the joy of forgiveness and embrace the amazing grace and love of Christ.

A Life of Repentance

When the great reformer, Martin Luther, nailed his Ninety-Five Theses to the church door at Wittenberg, the first of his theses was this, 'When our Lord and Master, Jesus Christ, said "Repent", He called for the entire life of believers to be one of repentance.'[4] Repentance and confession of sin must be the regular habit of our life as Christians. As long as we live in this world we will sin and we will need to repent and turn from that sin. When we repent, we are agreeing with God that we are sinners. We are acknowledging our sin, turning away from it, and turning toward our Savior. As the Apostle John wrote, 'If we say we have no sin, we deceive ourselves, and the truth is not in us. If we confess our sins, he is faithful and just to forgive us our sins and to cleanse us from all unrighteousness. If we say we have not sinned, we make him a liar, and his word is not in us' (1 John 1:8-10). That's why Jesus instructed the disciples to pray, 'Forgive us our sins, for we ourselves forgive everyone who is indebted to us' (Luke 11:4).

This life of repentance ought to push us to the cross and the grace of Christ. It ought to bring increased joy into our lives as well because we know how sinful we are and how amazing God's forgiveness is

---

4.　http://www.spurgeon.org/~phil/history/95theses.htm.　Accessed 2/28/15.

for us through Christ. Tim Keller writes, 'If regular confession does not produce an *increased* confidence and joy in your life, then you do not understand the salvation by grace, the essence of the faith.'[5] The ultimate end goal of repentance and confession is to be drawn deeper into God's grace, to know more of His great love for us, and to experience intimacy and communion with Him.

When hard and painful emotions visit our heart, we need to ask the Spirit to shine a light in our heart, asking Him to reveal to us the sin lurking within. We need to pray for eyes that see our desperate need for grace and forgiveness. We also need to pray for wisdom and discernment to know what aspect of our problem stems from sin and for the grace to repent of it. For though the pain of conviction hurts, its purpose is to bring healing and restoration as we confess our sins and receive forgiveness from our Savior.

For Your Heart

1. What sins do you need to repent for today? Read through Psalm 51 and claim it as your own as you come before the throne of grace in prayer and seek forgiveness for your sin.

2. Do you ever resist the pain of conviction?

3. Have you experienced 'good grief' before?

---

5.   Keller, Timothy. *Prayer: Experiencing Awe amd Intimacy with God* (New York: Dutton, 2014), p. 115.

PART 4

Living
the
Journey

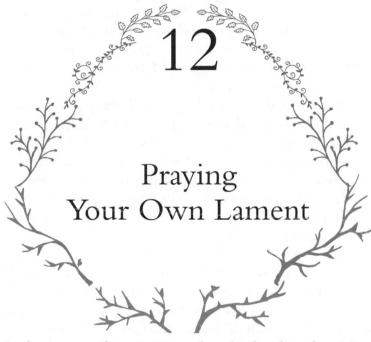

12

Praying
Your Own Lament

In the course of putting together this book and waiting to hear from the publisher whether they wanted to publish it or not, I found myself having to implement the very things I have shared here with you in these pages. During that time of waiting, my heart felt emotions such as fear, worry, and discouragement. The irony didn't escape me that I would have to do the very thing I had written in this book. And I did.

As I have looked back in my prayer journal and read what I wrote over those months of waiting, I saw my heart's cries poured out over the pages. I saw all the difficult emotions, the uncertainties I felt, and the questions I asked God. There were times when I wasn't certain that God wanted me to pursue writing a book. I struggled with whether I desired it more for myself or for Him. Was I seeking it for my own glory or His? As the months went on, I confessed the idols in my heart. I confessed the ways in which I had elevated my dream to write above my love for God.

The process of journeying through my own lament drew me deeper into God's grace. Though it was a difficult time, it was a beneficial time, for it brought about refinement and cleansing of sin. By the time I heard back from the publisher, I was at peace with whatever answer they gave. My heart had yielded to God. I found myself trusting God for whatever path He had for me.

My own journey of lament was a long one. There were many ups and downs. In fact, as I read through my prayers, I saw even more the depths of God's grace for me. After all, who but a loving God, rich and generous in mercy and grace, could listen to my cries and pleas day after day? I consider it a fruitful journey, not because it ultimately ended in my book being published, but because of what the Spirit did in my heart throughout those months.

In this chapter, I want to help you use what we've learned about the laments in your own prayer life. I want to encourage you to write your own laments. But first, let's look at a few things about prayer.

What is Prayer?

How would you define prayer? As believers, why do we pray? When you go to pray, do you consider it a chore to get over with? An item to check off your spiritual to-do list? A burden? Do you doubt its effectiveness? Do you ever enjoy your time of prayer? Do you ever feel drawn to pray?

Tim Keller describes prayer this way:

> Prayer is the only entryway into genuine self-knowledge. It is also the main way we experience deep change—the reordering of our loves. Prayer is how God gives us so many of the unimaginable things he has for us. Indeed, prayer makes it safe for God to give us many of the things we most desire. It is the way we know God, the way we finally treat God *as* God. Prayer is simply the key to everything we need to do and be in life.[1]

Prayer is key to our spiritual growth and vitality. In addition to God's Word, it's one of the ways we stay connected to the vine. It's the way we commune and communicate with our Father. Without prayer, we would be like ships adrift on the ocean. We would be lost, helpless, and alone.

As we have learned, the laments are the prayers of God's people. That's why Keller's description of prayer is so similar to what we've learned in our journey through the laments. Prayer teaches us about ourselves; it changes us and reorders us. It's also how we know God. It's how we receive from

---

1. Keller, Timothy. *Prayer: Experiencing Awe amd Intimacy with God*, p. 18.

Him what He has for us. It's how we rely on Him out of our utter dependency. When we pray, we treat Him as the sovereign God He is.

The laments are only one kind of prayer we could pray, so this chapter is not a lesson on prayer in general but on applying the principles we've learned about the laments into our own prayers. There are other important aspects to prayer that are outside the range of this book and I encourage you to study all that Scripture has to say about prayer, most notably, The Lord's Prayer in Luke 11.

Prayer and God's Word

Keller also says that prayer is the continuation of a conversation God has started in His Word.[2] God speaks to us through His written Word and we respond to what He says through our prayers.

God's Word is active and alive. Unlike other books we read, the Bible engages with our heart and soul and changes it. 'For the word of God is living and active, sharper than any two-edged sword, piercing to the division of soul and of spirit, of joints and of marrow, and discerning the thoughts and intentions of the heart' (Heb. 4:12). 'Since you have been born again, not of perishable seed but of imperishable, through the living and abiding word of God' (1 Pet. 1:23). 'Is not my word like fire, declares the LORD, and like a hammer that breaks the rock in pieces?' (Jer. 23:29). Though other books will affect us emotionally and get us to think about

---

2.   Keller, Timothy. *Prayer: Experiencing Awe amd Intimacy with God,*
       p. 83.

things a different way, no other book has the power of God's Word.

That's because God acts through His words. When He created the world, God spoke and the world came into being. When He said, 'Let there be light,' light appeared. He didn't speak and then go and make the light, His words created the light. Jesus proved His deity by speaking to the wind and rain and it ceased (Mark 4:39). Tim Keller says that 'if attended to with trust and faith, the Bible is the way to actually hear God speaking and also to meet God himself.'[3]

Our prayers then should arise out of our time in God's Word. Our prayers should be shaped by what we read in the Word. Our prayers should be a response to God's Word and to what God has revealed about Himself in His Word. While we don't need to literally read the Bible before every time we pray, our prayers should be molded by what we've learned in the Word.

When it comes to our study of the laments in the Psalms, what we've learned from the laments should shape and affect our own prayers to God.

Writing Your Own Laments

In this chapter, I want to take what we've learned from the laments and encourage you to write your own laments. I know, not everyone is comfortable with writing. I promise, you will not be writing an essay that will be graded. It doesn't need to be grammatically perfect nor even in complete sentences. This is a lament between you and God.

---

3. Ibid., p. 54.

Writing it down will help you to stay focused and remember all the elements of the laments. The act of writing engages your whole self so that you are fully immersed in what you are doing. If you get pulled away at some point, you can come back to it and pick up right where you left off. Writing down your lament also gives you an opportunity to look back at it later on and see how God has answered your prayer. Still doubtful? Try it at least once.

Begin by reading through one or more of the laments we have studied in this book. Then respond to what you've read in your own lament.

1. *Cry out to Your Heavenly Father*: The mere fact that we can bring our laments before God is a testament to the fact that God is God and we are not. When you cry out to Him in desperation, you are acknowledging your dependency upon Him. You are relying upon Him as your Father.

   The reason we can pray to God as Father is because of what Christ did for us at the cross. Simply saying His name in prayer is a reminder that we have been adopted into His family. As John Calvin wrote, 'Who would break forth into such rashness as to claim for himself the honor of a son of God unless we had been adopted as children of grace in Christ? ... By the great sweetness of His name he frees us from all distrust, since no greater feeling of love can be found elsewhere than in the Father.'[4]

---

4. Calvin, John. *Calvin: Institutes of the Christian Religion*, ed. John T. McNeill (Philadelphia, PA: Westminster Press, 1960), p. 899.

2. *Tell God where you are*: Begin your lament by telling God exactly where you are. As we learned in the laments, we can be honest and real with what is happening in our lives. Sometimes we think we have to clean ourselves up before we come to God in prayer. But we don't. Because of the gospel, Christ has already made us clean. We come to our Father in prayer the same way we come to the gospel, just as we are.

Paul Miller wrote, 'Jesus wants us to be without pretense when we come to him in prayer. Instead, we often try to be something we aren't. We begin by concentrating on God, but almost immediately our minds wander off in a dozen different directions. The problems of the day push out our well-intentioned resolve to be spiritual. We give ourselves a spiritual kick in the pants and try again, but life crowds out prayer. We know that prayer isn't supposed to be like this, so we give up in despair. We might as well get something done … We know we don't need to clean up our act in order to become a Christian, but when it comes to praying, we forget that … the only way to come to God is by taking off any spiritual mask. The real you has to meet the real God.'[5]

This is where we tell God exactly what we are feeling. Tell Him your worries. Tell Him all your fears. Tell Him the depths of your grief and despair. Tell Him that you feel forgotten, abandoned, and all alone. Tell Him that you are hurt and wounded.

---

5.   Miller, Paul. *A Praying Life: Connecting with God in a Distracting World* (Colorado Springs, CO: NavPress, 2009), pp. 30-31, 33.

3. *Ask questions*: Like the psalmist, ask God all the hard questions of life. Ask Him 'Why?' 'When?' 'How?' Ask Him those questions that have burdened your heart for so long.

4. *Repent*: As we just learned in the last chapter, confession and repentance are characteristic of the laments. If there is sin in your heart you need to confess, confess it. Perhaps the original pain you are feeling did not originate with your own sin; perhaps it was caused by the sin of another. But maybe you have responded to that pain in a sinful way. If so, confess it.

5. *Pray through the gospel*: We have also seen how the psalmist looked to God for salvation. He focused on God's love for him. This is where we pray through the gospel, reminding ourselves of who we are in Christ. Pray through and dwell on God's faithfulness for you in Christ. Pray about God's great love for you. Meditate on what it means to be forgiven and to be restored into right relationship with God.

6. *Ask for help*: What is it you want God to do? What do you need help with? Tell God exactly what you need. Pray for healing, for restoration in your relationships, for your needs to be met, for the needs of loved ones, for peace in your heart. 'And this is the confidence that we have toward him, that if we ask anything according to his will he hears us. And if we know that he hears us in whatever we ask, we know that we have the requests that we have asked of him' (1 John 5:14-15).

7. *Respond in praise and thankfulness*: This is where we turn our hearts toward God in trust.

Because of who He is and what He has done, we believe and trust that He is for us and He will never forsake us. 'What then shall we say to these things? If God is for us, who can be against us?' (Rom. 8:31). 'For he has said, "I will never leave you nor forsake you." So we can confidently say, "The Lord is my helper; I will not fear; what can man do to me?" (Heb. 13:5b-6). In response, we offer sacrifices of praise. In your lament, praise God for all He has done. Worship Him in love and thankfulness.

As I mentioned at the beginning of this chapter, I prayed through the laments in the course of writing this book. Here is one such prayer that I prayed. I give it to you only as an example. Your own lament will reflect your particular situation and emotions.

Father in Heaven,

I come before you today just as I am, weak, helpless, and completely dependent upon your grace. I am so thankful that because of Jesus, I don't have to wear a mask before you. I don't have to pretend or make myself something that I'm not. You accept me as I am because of the perfect blood of Jesus.

And so today, I come before you with my heart filled with so many different thoughts and emotions. I feel tense and uncertain about what I should be doing and where I should go. My mind is swirling with so many 'What ifs?' I feel so helpless and powerless. I am worried about what happens next and whether I am strong enough to face it. Deep down I wonder, how long will I be here? Will

I remain in this place of waiting forever? Why am I here to begin with? What's happening, Lord? But most of all, I wonder, where are you? Why haven't you responded to all my cries for help?

But even as I pray that, your Holy Spirit prompts my heart, reminding me of what is true. I know you are right where you've always said you would be. You've never left me and you will never forsake me. You are not deaf to my cries. In fact, you know the thoughts in my heart before I even think them. You know exactly what is happening, why I am here, and what is going to happen next. All things are in your sovereign care and control. There is nothing that happens outside your knowledge and will. Not even a hair can fall from my head without your permission and will. Nothing surprises you or takes you off guard. Including what's happening in my life right here, right now. You know why I am here waiting and you have promised to use it for your glory and my good.

Forgive me for all my doubts, worries, and fears. Forgive me for my impatience as I wait in this place. Forgive me for questioning the story you've written for me. Forgive me for not seeking your face and allowing the struggles before me to seem greater and stronger than your great grace and mercy for me. Cleanse my heart of all that keeps me from you. Help me to see the ways I have tried to be my own god and my own savior. Help me to see the counterfeit loves I have erected to worship and serve instead of you. Help me to see all those things I am clinging to right now that I think I must have to make me happy and help me to repent and turn from them.

My heart cries out with the father in Mark 9:24b, 'I believe; help my unbelief!' Help me to remember that it is good to wait for your salvation. As your word says, 'It is good that one should wait quietly for the salvation of the LORD' (Lam. 3:26). As I wait, help me to remember and dwell on the salvation you've provided for me through Christ. Help me to remember that the same grace that saved me at the cross is the same grace that strengthens and sustains me each day. That very same grace is at work in me even now, shaping me into the image of your Son. Help me to remember that no matter what happens, no matter my current circumstances, I am safe in the shelter of your wings. There is nothing that can separate me from you. For at the cross, you conquered my greatest fear – eternity apart from you. Because you gave the gift of Christ to me, I know that there is nothing I have to fear and no need you will not provide for me.

Grant me the joy that comes from knowing you and being known by you. Fill my heart with gospel joy. Strengthen me by your Word. May the words of the psalmist be true of me, 'I wait for the LORD, my soul waits, and in his word I hope' (Ps. 130:5).

Help me to remain faithful in this place of waiting. Help me to serve you and live for you even as I stand in this crossroad of my life. May I wait for you as long as it takes.

I pray all these things because of Jesus and in His name, Amen.

For Your Heart

1. How does praying in response to God's Word draw you closer to God?

2. What do you think about writing out your laments? Is it a practice you will continue?

3. How has studying the laments shaped how you cry out to God in prayer?

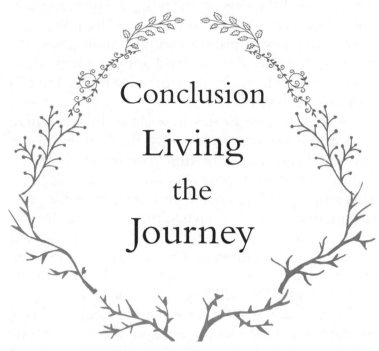

Conclusion
Living
the
Journey

Like any trip we take, we always have to return back home. The question is, will what we experienced and learned on our trip change us? Or will life just return to normal?

When the Visitors Return
When we began this journey, we started with those visitors, those emotions that hold us hostage and

control us. Remember them? What we've learned in this journey is that we don't have to be taken captive or led by our emotions. We've been set free by the blood of Christ from all captivity. We've been set free to now live in righteousness.

But because we live in a sinful world and still battle against the sins of our flesh, we have to daily remind ourselves of our freedom in Christ. We have to keep that key of promise with us at all times. We have to go to God in prayer and bring our laments to Him. We have to apply the truths we learned in His Word to our heart.

As our journey draws to a close, this is where I want to encourage you to live the journey of the laments. This is not a one-time journey. This must be a journey that we repeat over and over in our lives. This journey must become part of us in order for it to remain with us. We have to practice it and live by it. As we saw from our study of the laments, David wrote multiple laments. He turned to God time and time again, for various reasons and in multiple circumstances. We will have to do the same.

Every time we get a knock at the door and look through the little peep-hole and see one of our visitors standing there, we have to turn to what we have learned. We will have to cry out to God in our fear, our despair, our worry, our shame, our loneliness, and our desperation. We will have to seek Him as our Savior. We will have to rely on Him and His Word, preach the gospel to ourselves, and remember His faithfulness toward us. 'Those who sow in tears shall reap with shouts of joy!' (Ps. 126:5).

The truth is, we will see those visitors from time to time. For some of us, they may never truly go away. They might always linger off in the distance; just close enough for us to see them. This has been true for many heroes in the faith. For some of us, our emotions are like thorns in the flesh, a constant reminder of our need for grace. If you find yourself in that place, the laments may become not just an occasional way of life for you but a daily way of life. You will need to keep your eyes on Jesus, the author and perfector of your faith. 'Who for the joy that was set before him endured the cross, despising the shame, and is seated at the right hand of the throne of God. Consider him who endured from sinners such hostility against himself, so that you may not grow weary or fainthearted' (Heb. 12:2b-3).

Living the Journey in Community

We were created to live life in community. We were not meant to live in isolation but to journey together in the faith. God gave us the body of Christ, fellow brothers and sisters in Christ, who walk alongside us. We are to help each other, encourage each other, admonish each other, confess to each other, and carry each other.

Like a physical body, we move together as one unit. When one part feels pain, we all feel pain. When one part is suffering, we all suffer. Likewise, when one part rejoices, we all rejoice. And just as an arm can't go and live on its own apart from the body, may we not try to endure the pains of this life on our own apart from the body of Christ.

As we learned in the beginning of our journey, the laments were used in worship. They were sung together in community. As you move forward in your own journey of trusting God and relying on the gospel, sing your laments with others in your church community. Whether it is with your pastor or your prayer group or your best sister friend in Christ, sing your laments with them. Read this book with another sister in Christ. Walk this journey together, reminding and encouraging each other with the truth of the gospel.

And remember that one day, the winter of your sorrow will turn into spring. The sun will rise on the horizon, chasing away the darkness. Fear will give birth to laughter. All our hopes will be realized and made complete. 'And the ransomed of the LORD shall return and come to Zion with singing; everlasting joy shall be upon their heads; they shall obtain gladness and joy, and sorrow and sighing shall flee away' (Isa. 35:10).

Until that day,

Christina Fox

Also available from

Christian Focus Publications

THE ENVY OF Eve

FINDING CONTENTMENT IN A COVETOUS WORLD

MELISSA B. KRUGER

ISBN 978-1-84550-775-6

The Envy of Eve
Finding Contentment in a Covetous World

Melissa B. Kruger

This book guides readers to understand how desires grow into covetousness and what happens when this sin takes power in our hearts. Covetousness chokes out the fruit of the Spirit in our lives, allowing discontentment to bloom. The key to overcoming is to get to the root of our problem: unbelief-a mistrust of God's sovereignty and goodness. An ideal resource for deeper study or group discussion.

With empathy and grounded biblical insight, Melissa Kruger shows us the path to abiding joy amidst life's varied 'ups' and 'downs'.

Lydia Brownback
Author of *Contentment*, Wheaton, Illinois

In an age and culture where we all tend to have an overdeveloped sense of entitlement, this book makes a brilliant diagnosis that goes right to the heart of the problem.

Ann Benton
Author and family conference speaker, Guildford, England

With I've-been-there understanding and been-in-the-Word insight, Melissa B. Kruger helps us to look beneath the surface of our discontent, exposing our covetous hearts to the healing light of God's Word.

Nancy Guthrie
Author of *Seeing Jesus in the Old Testament Bible Study Series*

Melissa B. Kruger serves as Women's Ministry Coordinator at Uptown Church in Charlotte, North Carolina and is a speaker at various Christian conferences across the United States. Her husband, Michael J. Kruger, is the president of Reformed Theological Seminary in Charlotte.

God is my Strength

FIFTY BIBLICAL
RESPONSES TO ISSUES
FACING WOMEN TODAY

Patricia A. Ennis

ISBN 978-1-78191-642-1

God is My Strength
Fifty Biblical Responses to Issues Facing Women Today

Patricia A. Ennis

Women of the twenty-first century are faced with a myriad of issues. This book calls upon the Word of God to carefully answer 50 vital questions that every woman is facing today. Pat's loving approach will engage searching hearts and minds. She sensitively relates practical answers, keen guidance, and helpful approaches to steer them for a lifetime of honor to Christ.

... a treasure of information to help Christian women of all ages answer difficult life questions from a Biblical perspective and how to apply those Biblical principles in their lives daily. Women of all ages will benefit from the wisdom Dr. Ennis brings to the problems that women face in the 21st Century.

Kenda Bartlett
Executive Director, Concerned Women for America

... contains solid Biblical answers in a practical, readable volume. I highly recommend that 21st century women read God Is My Strength*, and give it to their friends and family members.*

Denise George
Author, teacher, speaker www.denisegeorge.org

... wipes away the stereotypes and misleadings. Using Scripture as her foundation, Dr. Ennis teaches women that biblical womanhood doesn't look like weakness or floral dress patterns, but intellect, courage and strength in the One who liberated us.

Chelsen Vicari
Author and Evangelical Action Director,
Institute on Religion & Democracy, Washington

Patricia A. Ennis is distinguished professor and director of homemaking programs at Southwestern Baptist Theological Seminary in Fort Worth, Texas and has authored and coauthored several books, including *The Christian Homemaker's Handbook*.

Christian Focus Publications

Our mission statement –

STAYING FAITHFUL
In dependence upon God we seek to impact the world through literature faithful to His infallible Word, the Bible. Our aim is to ensure that the Lord Jesus Christ is presented as the only hope to obtain forgiveness of sin, live a useful life and look forward to heaven with Him.

Our books are published in four imprints:

CHRISTIAN
FOCUS

Popular works including biographies, commentaries, basic doctrine and Christian living.

CHRISTIAN
HERITAGE

Books representing some of the best material from the rich heritage of the church.

MENTOR

Books written at a level suitable for Bible College and seminary students, pastors, and other serious readers. The imprint includes commentaries, doctrinal studies, examination of current issues and church history.

CF4•K

Children's books for quality Bible teaching and for all age groups: Sunday school curriculum, puzzle and activity books; personal and family devotional titles, biographies and inspirational stories – Because you are never too young to know Jesus!

Christian Focus Publications Ltd,
Geanies House, Fearn, Ross-shire,
IV20 1TW, Scotland, United Kingdom.
www.christianfocus.com